TESTIMONIES
OF
GOD'S LOVE

BOOK 2

Cover Design by

bespokebookcovers.com

TESTIMONIES

OF

GOD'S LOVE

BOOK 2

Del Hall and Del Hall IV

Acknowledgments

It is with the deepest love and gratitude we thank all those who contributed to this book. Their willingness to share some of their sacred experiences made this book possible. These testimonies show that so much more is possible in your relationship with God. We hope that reading them will inspire you to more fully accept the Hand of the Divine.

The authors would also like to thank all those who helped in the editing of this book. Emily and Anthony Allred, Catherine and David Hughes, and Kate Hall. Your keen eyes and thoughtful suggestions made a huge difference in the telling of these profound stories.

"The days of any religion or path coming between me and my children are coming to an end" saith the Lord

December 29, 2013

Table of Contents

Appendix

Foreword

One night when I was in my late teens I came out of my room and told my dad, "I feel like I am waiting for my spiritual teacher." Dad did not have an answer to the statement and it puzzled me as well. Deep inside I was waiting for someone and I did not even understand for what or why, but something was missing in life for me.

I really appreciate that as my parents followed their hearts they helped me follow mine. Dad had given me what I knew of God and religion. He brought me to church as a young child and then to a Self-Realization Fellowship, but I could not commit to a teaching. When I was nineteen my parents drove me from Michigan to the Catskills of New York to stay on an ashram for a month. After learning chants, doing yoga four hours a day, and eating a vegan diet I left no closer to the spiritual peace that I had never felt and yet I missed.

I was then given a beautiful dream. Although I did not know it at the time, it was an answer to my prayer for a spiritual teacher. This dream meeting and the fact that I was allowed to recall it was a profound gift from God. I hold this as one of my most sacred treasures. In the dream I was in a sea of golden light inside a giant golden bubble. There were smaller lights all around me like fireflies floating softly in a shimmering golden dome. A man came up to me and embraced me with open arms. I only saw him from his neck to his waist; he wore a long-sleeved blue garment. In that moment I experienced a love deeper, fuller, and more amazing than words can describe. I felt more complete, deeply joyful, and a sense of truly coming home. When I awoke it was clear that what I had experienced was real and that there existed a love that was unlike anything I had ever felt on this Earth. This was proof to me that there was more out there. There really was more to this life!

A few years after this dream my parents told me about Guidance for a Better Life. They had been to a couple retreats and had found something truly special. At first I thought the man from my dream was my future husband because the love I felt in his embrace was as deep and vast as the ocean. After attending a few retreats I learned that this person was indeed real and he could help me find the way to my true Heavenly Home again if I applied the necessary effort. His name is Del and he is the Prophet. He has the ability to speak for God and can teach the Language of the Divine on the outer during retreats and on the inner in the spiritual worlds.

I was then allowed to become one of His students. My relationship with the Prophet has changed my life from the inside out. He has given me, among other spiritual treasures, the deep peace I somehow knew was missing, but never felt until now. This peace comes from knowing that God loves me, just as I am. I know this with certainty from many experiences with the Light and Sound of God that were given to me by the Prophet. He is with me, in my heart, and therefore I am always Home.

My relationship with the Prophet has also given me a deeper gratitude and appreciation for life, family, friends, and even myself. This makes life a joyful adventure! *Gratitude is the secret of love.* This statement may seem simple, but it is a profound spiritual truth that has been a guiding light to me. On my hardest days, gratitude for my blessings from God is what gets me through. It opens the door of my heart and allows in God's ever-present Love and inspiration. As my heart opens I am able to give more love to others, which is one of my great joys.

You are Soul, a Divine spark of God. You have lived many lives and all the while you have not been alone. God always has one of His Prophets here on Earth to guide you, even if you have not been aware of his loving presence. To meet the Prophet, whether it is in dreams, contemplation, or in the physical, is a sacred blessing from God. May the pages in this book gently open your awareness to God's Divine Love for you. May they help you see the love that is inside and all around you, in this very moment, now, and always.

Carmen Snodgrass

Student at Guidance for a Better Life since 2007

Introduction

Welcome to book two of our "Testimonies of God's Love" series. Within these pages are fifty true stories that show the Hand of God reaching out to His children. This book, like our other books, celebrates the many varied ways God expresses His Love. God demonstrates His Love every day, but it often goes unrecognized. It is our hope that by reading these heart-warming testimonies you will learn to more fully recognize and accept God's Love in your own life. God's Love manifests in many ways from the dramatic to the very subtle. When you consciously recognize that God loves you, it can change your life. These authors have experienced this firsthand and are now building their lives on a solid foundation of knowing God personally loves them. They wish to pay it forward by helping you to do the same. Even if you recognize Divine love in your life, it is a profound blessing for God to remind you daily of His Love for you.

One of the first spiritual truths to consider, so you may more fully understand and enjoy this book, is that you do not "have" a Soul. The truth is, you ARE Soul. You are an eternal spiritual being within a temporal physical embodiment, which is to say you are Soul that has a body. In some of these stories the authors spiritually traveled into the Heavens. They traveled not in their physical bodies but as Soul. This is much like when Saint Paul shared that he knew someone who was caught up to the third Heaven. Soul can travel free of the body while still living. When the body does come to its end, the real you, SOUL, will continue on. Once again, you do not *have* a Soul; you *are* Soul that *has* a body. This seemingly simple change in perspective is actually of monumental significance. It is one of the core spiritual truths taught and experienced at Guidance for a Better Life and reflected within the testimonies of this book. When considered, or ideally experienced for yourself, it can open doors to even greater heights of wisdom, love, and understanding.

What then is Soul? In essence, Soul is an individualized piece of the Holy Spirit. We are not God, nor will we ever become God, but in a very real sense Soul is a piece of the Voice of God, the Holy Spirit. This is the true meaning behind the statement of being created in the image of God. Soul is a piece of the Holy Spirit, individualized and personalized through lifetimes of experience.

Life is busy and full of distractions making it easy to forget we are children of God, not just physical bodies. This is one reason why God always sends mankind His ordained Prophet. We need someone who sees clearly, can gently remind us that we are Soul, and who can help us soar free as spiritual eagles. God's Prophet can teach us the "Language of the Divine," the true native tongue of Soul. Then we may recognize and understand the Divine guidance that is always available for us! Fortunately, mankind is never without a Prophet. We are never alone. This is the greatest proof of God's Love for man — a continuous unbroken chain of divinely chosen and trained Prophets sent to help show us our way home to the Heart of God. As the current Prophet my father, Del Hall III, is now in this role and has been authorized to share God's Light, Love, and truth with the world.

This book is ultimately a celebration of God's Love for Soul and the many ways He expresses His Love. It is not an attempt to place a wedge between you and another spiritual teacher; it is intended to enhance whatever spiritual path you may be on, even if that is no path at all. As you may read in the Appendix, "What is the Role of God's Prophet?" you do not have to withdraw your love from a former Prophet (one who is no longer here in the physical) to benefit from being taught by the current Prophet. Having a guide who can teach you the Ways and Truths of God in both the inner spiritual worlds and also in the physical is such a blessing. Even so, if you are not comfortable accepting help from the current Prophet, there are still blessings within these pages for you. If you read this book with an open heart the testimonies within have the potential of greatly blessing you.

It is with great humility, reverence, and love that these authors share their experiences, blessings, and insights with you. They know God is truly reaching out through His Prophet to develop a more personal and loving relationship with each and every one of us. They know you too can experience even greater joy and abundance in your life by opening yourself to the truth within these pages — a truth that has the power to set you free and provide guidance for a better life.

Del Hall IV

4

Note to the Reader

All the authors who contributed to this book sing HU daily in spiritual contemplation. They tune in and raise up spiritually by singing HU, which makes them more receptive to the guidance and Love of God and God's Prophet. A basic understanding of both the role of God's Prophet and HU will help you more fully understand the "Language of the Divine" shared in this book. Please refer to the Appendix for an introductory understanding of God's historical line of Prophets and the role they serve.

HU is an ancient name for God that can be sung quietly or aloud in prayer. HU has existed since the beginning of time in one form or another and is available to all regardless of religion. It is a pure way to express your love to God and give thanks for your blessings.

Singing HU (HUUUUUU, pronounced "hue") serves as a tuning fork with Spirit that brings you into greater harmony with the Divine. We recommend singing HU a few minutes each day. This can bring love, joy, peace, and clarity, or help you rise to a higher view of a situation when upset or fearful.

1

A Beautiful and Familiar Sound

⁂

There are very few things of greater value we could share with you than HU. HU is an ancient name for God that can also be sung in loving gratitude as the purest of prayers. It raises you up and opens you up to be able to accept more of God's Love. The author of the following story shares her experience of singing HU for the first time in this life.

The first time I heard about the HU it was slightly out of my comfort zone. I had certainly listened to hymnals growing up and felt uplifted by some of them, but I had never heard about just singing a love song to God as a prayer. So when Del said he wanted to share something very special with us at the end of my retreat at Guidance for a Better Life, it was out of the box that I had about religion. I had tried chants before in yoga classes as a teenager and honestly did not really enjoy them. Would this be like those? No. Would singing this sound bring me closer to God? Yes. Would singing this song really express the love that I felt inside for the Heavenly Father? Yes. Would it be a true prayer? Yes.

I trusted Del. Everything he had taught me so far had rung true and I was willing to give something new a try. There was nothing to lose, and maybe there was actually something to it. And there was.

When the group of about twelve people started to sing HU I felt a little awkward at first, but the more I sang, the more I relaxed. I remember what Del had said before we started, it does not matter so much what your voice sounds like, it is about the love that you send when you are singing. And the more I relaxed, and focused on sending love in each HU, the more familiar it sounded. It was like I remembered this sound, even though I had never heard it before. We sang for about fifteen minutes, and it was the most beautiful song I had ever heard. I heard sounds within sounds. It actually brought tears to my eyes. This was Heavenly music. This was a completely new way for me to pray, to just say thank you and I love you to God. As we sang I just knew that God had heard me and felt such a deep peace knowing that. Something seemingly so simple had touched me deeply.

Now, after almost fifteen years of singing HU, I have grown to understand the value of the gift he gave me that day. Singing the HU has changed my life. I am so grateful to Del for teaching me this prayer. I am also grateful to have had the courage that day to try something new, to briefly step out of the little box I lived in, and experience a new way to express love to the Divine. The HU, a love song to God, so simple, yet so pure and beautiful.

Written by Molly Comfort

2

Divine Hand on My Back

This testimony is short and sweet ... not to mention profound. It shows there is no limitation to the ways God can comfort and guide His children.

I stopped at a restaurant with my daughter one evening and as we sat eating I was thinking about all of the things that I had going on in my life right then. I was getting remarried soon and there were a lot of things to do. I was not paying attention to my daughter but worrying about other things.

Just then I felt a hand touch my back. It pushed down gently between my shoulder blades. I looked around and nobody was standing behind me. There was not anyone near where we were sitting.

As the hand rested on my back I suddenly felt better, as if a weight had been lifted. I was able to set aside the other stuff and spend some quality time with my daughter. I believe this was the Divine giving me a gift of peace, reminding me where my focus should have been. I was able to listen to my daughter, who I do not see very often, and not later regret missing quality time with her.

I am so grateful for that amazing gift of love and comfort. Whenever I get stressed in life I try to remember that day and I begin to see things differently.

Written by Anthony Allred

3

Dream Warning Provides Protection

∾

There are times when one can be given advance warning in a dream. God can reach out and protect us by making us aware of upcoming danger. The following is a classic example.

In this dream I was driving to work on a familiar piece of highway. A large tractor-trailer came speeding up on my right and began coming into my lane. He apparently did not see me. The truck kept coming over and nearly pushed me into the guardrails on my left. I slowed abruptly to avoid a collision and began to move over into the right lane. At this point another car came up on my left and made a quick cut in front of me to get off the exit ramp.

In a short period of time I had two close calls where I had to react quickly to avoid an accident. I woke up and was still a bit shaken with a vivid recollection of this dream. On my way to work that morning on a very similar area as in the dream I saw a trailer truck coming up on my right. I remembered the dream so I slowed down well before he got alongside of me. He then swerved into the lane I had just been in. I was watching for a second car at this point and saw it come up on the left and make the abrupt cross over to exit the freeway. Both of these things happened just like in the dream. The only difference was that I was safely behind the truck and the second car, thanks to the warning in the dream.

I was very blessed and my day was so different because I was an observer of this situation from a safe distance. It was all due to the heads up I received in the dream. I was protected from a potentially tragic crash because I paid attention to this communication from God, took it seriously, and remembered it later in the day. Our dreams are real. If we dismiss or brush aside the information they contain we could be missing a valuable gift. A gift that could change our life or maybe even save it.

Written by Lorraine Fortier

4

The Beauty of Silence

Many folks pray to God but do not know how to "be still and listen" for a response. Each and every one of us has the potential to learn how to communicate with the Divine. It is at the core of what we teach seekers.

"Be still, and know that I *am* God." Psalm 46:10 KJV

During a retreat at Guidance for a Better Life Del said, "Spirit does some of its best work in silence." In the years before I heard him say this I had done a lot of talking to God, asking for one thing or another in prayer, but not nearly as much listening to what God had to communicate in response to my prayers. In the years since that retreat, some of the clearest communication that I have received from the Divine has come during moments of sitting in silence, very often right after expressing my love for God by singing HU. Sometimes the communication has come as a feeling, or better yet, a knowingness, within my heart. Other times I have been given a higher view of a situation that I am dealing with, or a deeper appreciation for the blessings already in my life. The Divine guidance in whatever form it takes has been there for me to "hear" and act upon. I was often deaf to this guidance until I learned to exercise the self-discipline to be still and listen, not just with my physical ears, but also with my heart.

I have experienced "listening" to be a true art form. On one visit to the retreat center, as I was unwinding from a long road trip my heart was opened by taking the time to stand still for a moment, let go of my thoughts, and enjoy a moment of inner silence as I appreciated the beauty of a late October afternoon, amid bright yellow leaves and a blue sky. Then something beautiful occurred. I experienced real peace come into me, a peace that set my mind and heart at ease. The peace was a part of something even more precious to me, the feeling of being loved. No one else was physically present, but the love was there, a gentle nurturing love.

It was in that silent moment and many since then that Spirit has done some of Its best work. It has been such a blessing to have been taught to devote at least a few minutes every day to being still and just listening. Thank you.

Written by Roland Vonder Muhll

5

It's a God Thing

The Divine seeks to bless us with insights and guidance in all areas of our life, even with finding the perfect job. The key is — can you hear and understand those gentle whisperings and will you trust and follow the timing?

Last summer I was down to the wire of needing a job. Right before leaving for a weekend retreat at Guidance for a Better Life I got a nudge to look at job listings. I opened up an ad on Craigslist for an administrative assistant. The job opening was for a part time position in a town thirty minutes away.

After the weekend I asked for guidance on the inner from the Prophet in writing a cover letter and tweaking my resume. Taking these with me it felt important to go and fill out an application at the Housing Authority, which was handling applications for the hiring company. When handing in the paperwork I inquired when the application paperwork would be picked up by the property management company and was told it would probably happen once the ad was done running.

While in town I visited some other businesses and left resumes. After listening to a very strong inner nudge to at least drive by the company's office to see where it was located, I decided to park nearby and commune inwardly with the Prophet. Asking on the inner what I should do, I got a very strong sense of a "can do" attitude and energy as a team, and that it would be important to hand a resume and cover letter directly to someone in the office. As I started to walk towards the office I got inner direction to not go there quite yet. Walking with and listening to the inner guidance I was reminded of the importance to detach from the outcome. It may have also been a timing issue.

When I got to the office the door was locked and the doorbell was lit up. I saw someone inside and got the "inner go ahead" to press the doorbell. A Vice President from the company came to the door. When I handed her my resume and letter for the job opening she had a very puzzled look on her face, and said that they did not have a job ad on Craigslist and that there was someone already in that position.

Well she continued to talk, she said that they were having a crisis at another location several hours away and that was taking their attention at the moment. Eventually she came back around to say that actually they were not happy with the current person in the position at the local property and had not yet addressed it due to the crisis situation. She mentioned that they hire through a specific temp agency. I told her that was interesting, as that is the company I currently work for! She came up with the idea that perhaps it would be an easy transfer. Then she said she knows that you are not supposed to talk about religion in the industry, but this is a "God thing!" I agreed with her that it definitely was a "God thing!"

As I was returning home I received a call to set up an interview and chose the earliest available date, which was the next morning. By the following Monday I was working in that position! It evolved from no ad, no job, to starting to work the following week! The temp agency says they never use Craigslist to advertise and no one has taken credit for writing the ad. The ad was written for me, tailor made to match my work skills and experience. In my heart I am very grateful to God. Getting the job is just one layer of the blessings. My gratitude is especially deep for the teamwork and relationship that I experienced with the Prophet. A loving relationship with the Prophet of God is priceless and affects all areas of life in a positive way.

Another precious layer, God read my heart. For the past several years it has been my dream and goal to work and live in that town, but the goal seemed so far away from fruition. God's plan and timing is impeccable. All sorts of details, large and down to very small, have come together in this job and it has been a perfect match for me and for the company. Things have worked out way beyond any possible planning on my own. Truly we are loved by God, and the love and blessings are available and showered upon us. It took the teachings of the Prophet to be aware of and to see and experience God's love for me.

Written by Jan Reid

6

A Child of God is Born

*Sometimes God pulls back a curtain allowing us to
experience the spirituality of a situation. The following
is a beautiful testimony of witnessing the sacredness of
childbirth. It is at this moment that Soul enters
the body and a new adventure begins.*

How grateful I am for my children, three gifts
that God has bestowed upon my wife and I.
What were once happy "additions" to the family
are now integral parts that I would not want to
imagine our lives without. Each of my children's
births was a precious and sacred moment, but it
was the birth of my eldest child that gave me a
glimpse into the Divinity that was clothed in each
little bundle of joy.

The morning my oldest child was born, I stood
in the delivery room experiencing all the
nervousness and excitement of a first-time dad-
to-be. My mind raced forwards and backwards as
the moment crawled nearer and nearer.

Because I was at the front of the bed, ready to offer sips of water and cold washcloths to my wife, I could see everyone else in the room. Several people, including the doctor, head nurse, and various other nurses and assistants popped in and out. Time seemed to slow to a freeze and I watched, with this sort of detached viewpoint, a panorama of the other people there.

There was what I can only describe as a reverent anticipation bubbling up in the room. Everyone - it seemed like a lot more than the three or four individuals there - seemed riveted on this sacred moment. There was an overwhelming reverence for Soul permeating the air. A spark of God was about to don another body, take its knocks, learn its lessons, and continue on Its journey home to the Heart of the God. I believe each person there, whether conscious of it or not, was recognizing Soul – the Divine spark about to be housed in a tiny little body - but also which lived in each other and in themselves. Each in his or her own way recognized that the source of this spark of life was God.

While my wife, the doctor, and several nurses prepared for the imminent birth, a young nursing assistant stood in the middle of the room unconsciously rocking back and forth, in a slow cadence to some distant rhythm only she could hear. She hugged herself instinctively, as if rocking an invisible baby in her arms. It was hard to say if she was imagining comforting the baby about to be born or herself. Maybe both.

When my son finally arrived, I moved into position to "catch" him. I witnessed a ball of glowing light so intense and brilliant it became hard to see anything else. I immediately recognized this Soul as someone I had loved dearly before. Watching Soul enter the body was breathtaking. The doctor and nurses helped guide his tiny body into my arms. I was holding him when he took his first breath in this body, before surrendering him to my wife's welcoming embrace. The recognition between mother and son seemed apparent as well.

In my years at Guidance for a Better Life, Del has repeatedly led me to experiences that have shown me there is so much more to us than just our bodies – much more than just the parts we can normally see. I believe I witnessed a glimpse of that in my son as he was being born, a glimpse into the Divine essence of our being, which is born into this world to learn, to love, and to attempt to pick up the trail back to Its eternal Home.

Written by Chris Comfort

7

Bravo the Love Cat

One of the main reasons you are here on Earth is to learn more about giving and receiving love. The two are inseparable. The following is a beautiful story, full of wisdom, about how a cat helped someone grow in this most important of understandings.

A few years ago I was lonely and ached for love, but did not realize that I needed to give love more than I needed to receive love. I had fallen into the trap of thinking about myself too much. Rather than trying to help someone else I looked to fill my own needs. It became a vicious cycle where the more I wanted and tried to get love, the further away it seemed. During retreats at Guidance for a Better Life I have heard Del say many times that the best way to get love is to give love. While I understood the words, I was not practicing them.

Then, during a retreat, Del suggested that I get a cat. Maybe having something to love, even a cat, would help. To me this suggestion felt like a lifeline, or one of those "In Case of Emergency" boxes, only this one containing a cat. I love how Spirit works. Where the human solution might consist of struggle or hardship, the Divine suggests a warm furry friend.

I went to the animal shelter praying for help from my inner guide, the Prophet, to find the cat that was right for me. I walked slowly through the aisles in the cat rooms, stopping to take out and spend time with one cat after another. Finally I got to the last row but still had not found my cat. I wandered into another room to hear an employee saying, "If you are looking for a cat who wants to sit in your lap and be loved all day, these are not the cats for you." When I asked her where I would find those cats, she said that I needed to meet Bravo.

We returned to that last row and I met Bravo, who was as sweet and loving as she described. We sat and enjoyed each other's company for quite a while. When I started to worry that someone else might adopt him if I did not bring him home right away, I knew I had found my cat.

Soon after, I was at home on the couch with Bravo feeling so much love for him. I felt like a light finally came on in a room I had not even realized was dark. Pouring love onto my cat is even more satisfying than the love he gives me. I was filling a need I did not even realize I had. Love is like breathing; you have to exhale before you can take the next breath. Having him to love changed everything.

Every day, Bravo opens my heart, and not only to him. Because I am open to give and receive love with him, I can accept love from friends, family, and even the Divine, which makes me want to give even more love. Thus begins an upward spiral of ever-expanding love and joy. Loving him opened a door to accept the love that had surrounded me the whole time.

There is a ball of God's Love that lives in my house. It is disguised in black and white fur that makes it look like a cat, but I know the truth. He has brought so much love into my life, so many blessings. I know he is a gift from God.

Written by Jean Enzbrenner

8

Broken Neck Healed by the Light of God

❦

In this story of protection and being healed by God's Light, there is much to be grateful about. It shows there is no limit to what God can do, including healing someone before the injury even occurs.

Last summer I was in a car accident. The accident itself was a miracle because no one was seriously injured. I was run off the highway, crossed the median, and stopped right before oncoming traffic. The other car was pushed back into our traffic lanes but was not hit by other cars. I drove home that evening and went to get an x-ray the next day just to make sure I was not injured. The doctor came in and told me "don't move," a C-collar was placed on my neck and I was laid down. I thought it must be some kind of joke as I had been walking around all night. The doctor said that the x-ray showed a fractured C6 vertebra, a broken neck. She showed my husband the x-ray and he could visibly see where my bone was misplaced. I was transferred to the emergency room, and as I lay there for a few hours, I was praying to God, as were my family and friends. Doctors were discussing a possible surgery for that evening. I had a CT scan to get a better image and the doctor said "It must have been a bad x-ray; you don't have a fractured neck." My husband and I looked at each other and knew, it was not a bad x-ray, it was a healing. My husband had seen the x-ray with his own eyes.

Not long after this I was attending a HU sing at Guidance for a Better Life when the Prophet, my spiritual guide, took me back to an experience on the inner that I had earlier in the year, before my accident. During this experience, I was touched by God's Light! I was bowed in reverence as God's Light shone down on the back of my neck. To be touched by the Light of God was an amazing life changing experience! I know God loves me! I felt so much love, joy, warmth, peace, and strength during this experience that I was not paying attention to where I was touched. I was focused on the immense blessing it was that I was actually being touched by God's Light. It was not until I was shown this experience again that I realized I was specifically touched right at my C6 vertebra. I was immediately taken back to the accident and saw a direct connection between these two experiences. I know the Light of God touching my neck that day was a healing. Wow!

I am so very grateful and appreciative for the Love of God and I am blessed to see God's Love throughout my daily life.

Written by Emily Allred

9

The Flute of Heaven

My father, Del Hall III, has led many a seeker on journeys into the Heavenly realms during both waking and sleeping states to experience the Holy Ghost - the Sound and Light of God. These travels help shed light on your true nature as a spiritual being and pull back the curtain on the Heavenly Kingdom.

When I was a young boy my parents played traditional Japanese flute music each night to help me fall asleep. The gentle melodies seemed to be the only thing that could coax me into rest. The soothing compositions brought a peace that was largely absent during my waking hours. I looked forward each night to the familiar sounds. I am so grateful that they played this beautiful music. But nothing could compare to the music of the flute I heard in a dream, years later.

This dream was given to me seven years ago. I awoke in full consciousness to find myself in a region of pure light. As far as the eye could see was vibrant, pulsating, yellow light emanating from a central figure. Closer to the figure the light became ever more pure, whiter and whiter, finer and finer. The light itself seemed dynamic and alive. In the middle of this light-filled universe sat Del Hall, my spiritual guide, a true Prophet of God. He played a traditional wooden flute.

His music filled this world, the most beautiful sound I have ever heard! As he played, I did not know if a minute had passed, or a day, or a month, or a year. I could not tell distance either: Del sat in the center of this beautiful world, but was he three feet away, or three miles? There was no way to tell, for there was no matter in this realm. It was only the pure Light and Sound of Heaven. As he played the music brought peace that far surpassed anything I had experienced before. This peace entered me and filled me, and it lives in my heart to this day. It is a gift that keeps on giving. Simply placing my attention on this dream brings back the serenity of this beautiful music. This is the peace that surpasses all understanding spoken of in the Bible. Upon waking, I was overcome and gave thanks for this incredible experience.

This was more than a dream. It was a journey into Heaven. The fifth Heaven, where only purity and goodness and light exist. There was no time, no near or far, no shadow, no high or low. There was only the Source, and the Light and Sound of God. In the Bible, Saint Paul said he knew a man who was caught up to the third heaven (Second Corinthians 12:2). This means that there is at least a first heaven, a second, and a third. This dream took place in the fifth Heaven, where there is no matter, only Light and Sound. There is no evil, only goodness and light. As a Prophet of God, Del Hall is able to take his students into the Heavens in full consciousness. To the fifth Heaven and beyond.

This dream motivated me to continue my spiritual path without hesitation. It showed me that Del was no *ordinary* preacher or spiritual teacher. Something I had already known in my heart, but this left no doubt. He is the modern Prophet of God, able to share the Light and Sound of God. Following his teachings and guidance had led to this experience, and the understanding of it.

Many have heard references to the Light of God. Few have heard of the Sound, the Heavenly white music. Yet scattered references

33

to it exist in the various world scriptures. Having experienced it, I can tell you that it is unlike anything else. It is more than "music." It is the voice of God, and it carries all the qualities of God's love. Peace, love, mercy, joy, and more! It can be experienced by man today. It is this sound, this beautiful Sound of God that can carry Soul back to its eternal home.

Written by David Hughes

10

Help Finding a New Home

For those who understand and pay attention to the "Language of the Divine," life can be a joy to live. Whether through a nighttime dream or an awake dream this loving guidance is available at every step on the journey through life. It provides the insight we need for smooth passage and serves as a constant reminder — we are loved and we are not alone.

A couple of years ago my fiancé and I decided to relocate from Massachusetts to Virginia. After identifying the general area we felt would be a good place to live and build a business, we began our search for a house to rent.

Two months prior to our anticipated move we flew to Virginia with a list of houses we hoped to see in our short visit to the area. On our way to the first house on our list, a "for rent" sign in front of another house caught my eye. The front door was wide open so we stopped. The owners happened to be packing their car with a few last things before moving to Massachusetts, of all places. We were met with a warm welcome and gracious offer to be shown around. It turned out that the house was not right for us, but the experience stood out as an awake dream, a communication from the Divine, reminding us to stay flexible where our plans were concerned and alert to other "open doors" of opportunity that may catch our attention along the way.

This sense of adventure stayed with us as the day unfolded. Everything just flowed. Planned stops interwoven with unexpected detours and surprises as if we were being led from one open door to the next. Toward the end of the day I followed an inner nudge to explore a neighborhood on the other side of town where, as far as we knew, there were no available houses for rent. To our surprise we came upon a "for rent" sign in front of a gray house with an unusual roofline. When we pulled up, the license plate "OPNLOCK" on the vehicle in front of us caught my attention. The front door was wide open and workmen were coming and going. One of them directed us to the landlord who happened to be working on-site that day. Although the house had just been rented, when he heard what we were looking for, he suggested another house he had nearby which was not quite ready yet. As it turned out it was the perfect house for us, in the perfect location, at the perfect price.

Later that night as I leafed through my dream journal before bed I came across a sketch I'd scribbled upon waking from a dream a few days prior. It depicted a gray house with an unusual roofline located where two main routes intersected, an exact description of the house where we met our future landlord that day. To me this was an added layer of reassurance that we were moving in the right direction, in harmony with God's plan, as we embarked on this major life change.

At the end of the day any worry I had been carrying about our upcoming move was replaced with trust and a sense of adventure for what lay ahead. Along with this, a gentle knowingness that our efforts, coupled with an openness to being led by the Divine along the way, would result in everything working out for the best. Which it has, in every way.

The golden thread of God's Love weaves an abundant life for each of us. Developing our own personal relationship with the Divine is the key that opens the door to a truly blessed life.

Written by Sandra Lane

11

Hiking With Mom in Heaven

It is a sacred opportunity and blessing to visit with a loved one who has passed away. Because we are personally known and loved by God, sometimes God will answer additional prayers of the heart during these reunions. In the following example the author had the chance to experience the trip he had wanted to take with his mother.

My mother passed away recently at age eighty-eight. She had a strong faith and often spoke joyfully about going to Heaven when her time came. In fact, she specifically requested that my three brothers and I sing at her funeral the old hymn, "When We All Get to Heaven."

She had been widowed at age fifty-five when my father had a massive heart attack. She never remarried. She continued to teach elementary school for ten more years and then retired to enjoy a life of volunteer work and traveling. Upon returning from one of her trips to Ireland, she said she wished I could have been there to hike with her in the beautiful countryside. I wished I could have been there too!

The last few years I watched her body decline, but as Soul, she remained her delightful, joyful self. As she needed more and more help with daily living we spent more and more time together. The bond between us grew through many weeks of cancer treatments and hospitalizations. When she breathed her last breath, it was bittersweet. I know she is finally where she longed to be, and yet I miss her.

Soon after her passing I was blessed to be at Guidance for a Better Life. A group of students and Del, the Prophet, were singing HU, a love song to God. During the silent time after singing, Del appeared spiritually in front of me on the inner and took me to see my mother! She was standing in a beautiful green meadow. The day was unusually bright and clear, with a hint of cool breeze. Mom's appearance was just as it was in her middle adult years, still with the natural color in her hair. She was wearing brightly colored clothes and sunglasses, with a big smile. She was so happy to see me and I was so happy to see her. She beckoned me with her arms to come walk with her. We hiked along together through the meadow and up a light brown dirt trail up into the surrounding hills. As we went higher we saw the beauty of the meadow from above. It was more beautiful than I could ever imagine Ireland to be. We spoke no words, sharing love and joy in our hearts to be hiking there together, fulfilling our wish from many years ago.

When my awareness returned to the room where I was sitting, I was glowing with love and gratitude for Del, a true Prophet, for taking me there. What an amazing gift! I now know for sure that mom really is happy and well, and that she still loves me dearly.

My brothers and I look forward to singing joyfully at her memorial service, "When we all get to Heaven, what a day of rejoicing that will be, when we all see Jesus, we'll sing and shout the victory!" I have no doubt she will be singing with us!

Written by Paul Harvey Sandman

12

Sound That Changed Me

There is a very big difference between having a relationship with God based on love versus one based on fear. While there is a call for reverence, to live with a constant fear or worry of damnation closes our heart and is counterproductive to God's will. God desires to bless and guide us but cannot deliver these to a heart closed by fear. If you wish to nurture a more loving relationship with Our Father, the HU Love Song is one of the best ways to do so.

When I was growing up I lived in a rural town and I went to small church with my family. I was told that God loves us and that Jesus loves us also. I knew this in my heart but always knew there was more. Around twenty years ago, when I started attending retreats at Guidance for a Better Life, I learned a love song to God. Before that I only knew how to respect God or to fear Him as the Bible says. At the retreat center I learned a beautiful song called HU. I was told by Del, my teacher, that it is a love song to God and when you sing it you are focusing on sending love to God with all of your heart. Learning this changed my life. I have experienced, when singing HU, that my heart opens and I am filled with gratitude.

One weekend at the retreat center I had an experience while singing HU. Del was leading the retreat and we began singing HU. As I started to sing my heart really opened to know that I was singing a love song to God, I could feel the love that I had for God, and it felt strong. By having this experience, I realized that it was a gift. I realized to give love back to God and tell Him that I love Him is one of the most loving things that I could do. I felt that my heart naturally wanted to do this. At that moment I was so grateful to be able to sing HU! While singing HU I experienced in some way that God was blessing others.

When singing I could feel and hear the sound of HU go up to God. This experience was a knowing, not something that I could mentally wrap my head around, but a feeling that was true in my heart. Spiritually I could see a golden ring go around the world and shower it with love, God's Love. God's Love went out to people going about their everyday life just touching them with a gift of light. As I saw that, it made me want to give more. The sound of HU surrounded me, also hearing the sound of everyone else at the retreat singing HU and knowing that they had the same intention, filled me with peace and love. That peace was palatable. I was so grateful for this experience and grateful to Del, a Prophet of God, for teaching me this love song.

This experience was a blessing, and as I reflect back in time, it reminds me that we are loved, God really loves us, and He hears us! God gave us a song to sing. By singing it everyday it opens my heart, it opens my heart to the love that I have for God, and the love that He has for us. It also reminds me that I have love to give to others. Thank you Del for teaching me the greatest song of all, HU.

Written by Golder O'Neill

13

A Golden Lifeline of Love

*We are living on Earth during unprecedented times.
The opportunity for spiritual growth in this lifetime is
almost unlimited. God is directly seeking a more
personal relationship with each and every one of us.
The hand of the Divine is reaching out — will
you accept it?*

I was at a spiritual retreat at Guidance for a Better Life. Del was guiding us in a spiritual exercise that helped us tune out distractions of the outer world and go on the inner to seek guidance, counsel, and wisdom from the Holy Spirit.

We opened our hearts to Divine Love by thinking of things in our lives that we were truly grateful for and then we sang HU, a beautiful love song to God. I felt totally safe and was receptive to whatever experiences and adventures might come. I could see violet and blue lights swirling in my inner vision. My eyes were closed so I knew the light was not physical in nature. This was spiritual light.

This inner vision became very bright. There was a beam of white light that came into view and out of this came "golden threads." One of these golden threads was being offered to each of us. It was a gift of love direct from God. We were told that if we wanted we could choose to accept it. I did. I reached out, took hold of it, and tied it under my arms like a harness. I wanted to make the most of this opportunity and I wanted this connection to stay secure. I knew that what was being offered was priceless beyond my understanding, and I never wanted to let go of It, or It let go of me. If I ever encountered difficult times or got lost in the passing parade – the non-eternal distractions of the material world; this golden cord could be a lifeline and help me find my way back home.

Even though I have not always been conscious of it being there, I know this has been a spiritual lifeline for me and has blessed me in so many ways. It is a connection between my heart and God's Heart. The love that flows through it goes both ways. In looking back I see it was an offer to have a personal relationship with God. This relationship has grown into a true love. This love connection nourishes and sustains me every day. It has brought comfort, peace, and clarity during challenging times and has helped me learn and grow from those lessons of living. It makes "ordinary days" extra-ordinarily satisfying and full of joy, wonder, and richness. I treasure this experience and so appreciate this precious gift of God's Grace and enduring Love.

Written by Lorraine Fortier

14

Breadcrumbs From God

Sometimes even a seemingly simple dream contains great wisdom. Through practice we can learn to glean the pearls of wisdom out of our dreams. Even better yet, we have the opportunity for the one who taught us in the dream to help us understand its meaning. This ability to teach us in both the dream state and waking state is key to the opportunity for spiritual growth with God's Prophet as our guide.

During a retreat at Guidance for a Better Life I had a dream that seemed simple at first but was full of images that were meaningful to me. Even a few moments of a dream can contain a profound message from the Divine. In the dream I was standing in the sleeping loft of a cabin, looking down into the kitchen below. A woman was frying two eggs and I was upset because I did not think she should. Then I saw Del carrying a tray of breadcrumbs outside. Seeing Del in the dream got my attention; seeing him is always significant. When I shared the dream the next morning Del helped me see how this seemingly simple dream contained a key to spiritual growth.

In the loft with the higher view was Soul, my true self. As often happens in dreams the woman in the kitchen was also me, but the lower, human side of me. Through the eggs the dream showed me that my actions nourished my lower physical self, but not Soul, my higher eternal self. Like the body needs food, so does Soul. Whatever draws one closer to or into alignment with God nourishes Soul. It could be singing HU, a love song to God, practicing gratitude, reading scripture, or being aware of the Prophet with me spiritually throughout the day.

However, thoughts of fear, worry, or self-doubt do not nourish us but instead drain our energy and deplete us. That is what Soul, the real eternal me, did not want my lower self to do. Yet I did often listen to my worries and fears. By doing so I could not hear God or God's Prophet whispering a solution to each of my concerns. My thoughts depleted me, affected the quality of my life, and even jeopardized an opportunity for spiritual growth.

The breadcrumbs Del carried outside were all that remained of a spiritual feast; even the opportunity for crumbs could slip away. Every retreat is a golden opportunity for Soul to learn and grow that comes, not once in a lifetime, but once in many lifetimes. Without nourishment, Soul cannot learn and grow. I could not go any further until I learned to control my thoughts and focus on what nourishes Soul.

It would have been easy to overlook this dream and not bother to write it down or share it. It seemed so simple, yet the message was significant and of great importance to me.

Written by Jean Enzbrenner

15

A Drop of God's Love

There is no limit to what even a single drop of God's Love can do. It can move mountains, part seas, change destinies, heal relationships, and so much more. It is possible to visit the source and drink from this well.

I have learned by experience that it is entirely possible to perceive some of the wonders of God's Heavens while still walking the Earth. My body cannot visit these realms of God, but I, Soul, can do so with the help of my spiritual guide and teacher. He can and does take me on journeys beyond the confines of space and time even while my body sits upon the ground, or in a favorite chair.

After singing HU, an ancient love song to God, for quite some time, I had the opportunity to go on one such journey. I was led to what seemed like a vast ocean. What appeared at first to be water was actually unlimited quantities of love and mercy. Kneeling before this vast ocean of love and mercy, I knew that I was in the Presence of God, the creator of all things. The waters, and even what seemed to be the sands of the beach, were alive, energetic, glittering gold, sometimes blue with hints of other colors. There I experienced a deep peace and contentment, a sense of completeness far beyond what I had previously known. The living waters gently caressed me, like the hand of a father welcoming home a child who has been gone a long time.

Del, my teacher, suggested I dip one finger in this ocean and consider how much of God's Love is contained in a single drop. I was asked to consider how much impact a single drop of this Divine Love could have upon this Earth.

So I dipped my finger in this Heavenly Sea, and I experienced the living water glowing gold, tinged with other rich colors. It flowed around my finger, not as though pulled by gravity, but with loving intent and creative purpose, glowing intensely and spreading a strong but gentle warmth through my finger and entire being. Suddenly my consciousness expanded to see some of the potential of that little bit of Divine essence. In an instant I saw that this little drop of God's Love could heal countless broken hearts and comfort countless hurting Souls. It can change the course of one's destiny, averting tragedy and bringing peace instead. There are no limits to what God's Love can do, though we may limit it with what our minds believe to be impossible.

So, dear reader, I testify to you that there is even now a Prophet of God who may take you to this same Divine well, that you may also experience and drink deeply of these living waters. God is real, and God's Love is available to you in quantities beyond measure. Drink deeply of God's Love, and share the peace and joy you find in this with those you love and meet. Thank you for the privilege of allowing me to share my experience with you.

Written by Timothy C. Donley

16

The Moment That Changed Me

There are so many people who do not feel worthy of God's Love. Sad as that is, it is understandable when you recognize how much guilt is "in the air down here." It rests like a heavy fog over everything obscuring the truth. The truth that even though we all fall short on occasion and have moments we wish we had done better, we are still loved by God. What a blessing it is when the Prophet gently blows away the fog.

We were being guided through a spiritual exercise during a retreat at Guidance for a Better Life. During the exercise I had experienced God's Love. When I began to share my experience, I had trouble saying, "I am loved, God loves me." I truly did not feel worthy of God's Love. How could God love me when I did not pray to Him regularly, when I did something wrong, when I held anger for a family member or co-worker, or when I had a bad day and was grouchy to the people around me?

I have learned that even when I am not having a "good" day that I am loved! I am Soul, a child of God, and nothing changes that fact. My human shortcomings do not change the fact that God loves me just the way I am, faults and all. "I am loved, God does love me." Just as He loves every one of us. Sometimes life has a way of pulling the chair out from under us and we each react differently. Some lessons are learned easier than others. God would not have created me if I did not have a purpose and He did not love me. During my debrief the more Del suggested that I repeat out loud "GOD LOVES ME, I AM LOVED," the deeper it sank into my heart. I not only said those words, I believed them with every fiber of my being. I know God loves me.

Written by Rebecca Vettorel

17

Night School and Beyond

*What child never dreamed of soaring free like a bird?
What adult has had a flying dream and not been able
to share it at work the next morning without a twinkle in
their eye? It is in us deep and comes from our deep
knowing that we are more than these physical bodies.
We are Soul, and as Soul, we are free. We can take a
break from these "earth suits" and explore
the greater worlds of God.*

As a child I remember wondering what it would be like to go into outer space. I wondered if there was more than just what we could see with our physical eyes. Where do people go when they die? Is there really a Heaven? I would imagine what it might look like. These questions were answered for me at a young age. Yes, *there is more.*

At the age of seven I remember leaving my physical body at night as I would lay down for sleep. I would slip into another dimension outside of the physical world and fly around. We lived on a wildlife refuge center with over three hundred acres of beautiful property. There were rolling grass hills, ponds, and wildlife such as deer, Whooping Cranes, Canadian Condors, and other endangered species. This was a government owned property we lived on in the 1970's. My father worked there and we lived on the estate as part of the employment arrangement. As Soul I flew outside our home just above the grass and over the ponds at high speeds without the entanglement of my physical body. It was exhilarating and the freedom I felt was incredible.

The ability to spiritually travel left me at the age of ten, and it was not until I began attending retreats at Guidance for a Better Life in my early thirties, that I resumed those kinds of experiences. But now I had help and was able to be guided to much greater heights with a sense of purpose. I am able to go to "night school" as my physical body rests.

Del, a true Prophet of God, invited us to a temple of God's wisdom during a spiritual retreat I attended. The temple was in a city on Venus. The only way to get there was via spiritual travel as Soul. I was very excited about this and accepted the invitation. Del came in his radiant light Soul body and put his hand out to me. I went with him to this beautiful temple. He introduced me to the temple guardian there. We went to a waterfall of spiritual light and sound and here the image of a book sat on a pedestal. When I looked into the book I saw the word "love." I stepped into the waterfall of God's Light and Sound and I was filled with love, wisdom, peace, joy, and more. This was one of my first experiences of spiritual travel with an experienced guide who could escort me. My childhood dream of going to "outer space" was answered. I now knew that Del was teaching me God's ways and that this was a path of love. I knew that I had found my teacher.

After the experience at this temple, whose name means House of Liberation, I began having spiritual travel experiences regularly. In the dream state I meet with the Prophet. He takes me to whichever temple is right for me and I have a lesson in the form of an inner experience. I have had many dream experiences at various temples of God's wisdom, from temples on the physical plane, to recently being taken to a temple at the twelfth Heaven, in the Heart of God.

What is so special about these experiences is that I know that I am Soul first. I am not just my physical body. I have learned the value of investing in the eternal. These teachings are eternal and we can access them via invitation from a Prophet of God. I have learned much more than if I had been limited to an outer teacher only. We can learn on the outer and on the inner from the Prophet. To me that is very special and I am grateful for that privilege.

Written by Tash Canine

18

Reunion With Childhood Dog

❦

*The greatest lessons pets help us with are in learning
more about giving and receiving love. They also teach
us about responsibility, the pain of loss, and in the
following story, reincarnation. Animals are Soul too,
and as such, their journey carries on
beyond a single lifetime.*

When I was in kindergarten my mother and
stepfather drove me to a house where a new
litter of puppies was born. When I saw the
puppies my mother asked me to choose one. I
distinctly remember knowing I should kneel
down away from the pack and wait. When I did
one of the small puppies made her way towards
my lap. We named her Daisy. She was a mixed
breed that was mostly Golden Retriever.

Daisy became such a loving and faithful
companion throughout my childhood years. On

Saturdays, after doing my chores, I would collect my allowance and my friend and I would take our bikes into town several miles away. Daisy would often follow us. During visits to libraries, department stores, 7-Eleven, and the movie theater she would wait patiently outside. At the end of the day when we were going back home, Daisy would run in front of the bikes leading the way. She would occasionally look back at me as if to say, "hurry hurry, I'm hungry and want to get home!" In my early teenage years I moved from my mother's to live with my father near Washington, DC. My mother moved out to Phoenix, Arizona and took Daisy with her. I always wondered how Daisy felt about my leaving and if she missed me like I missed her. Sadly she passed away before I was ever able to see her again, leaving a painful spot in my heart.

About eighteen years later I moved to Tucson, Arizona with a girlfriend I had at the time. Coming back from a late night martial arts class my headlights flashed on a pair of eyes as I pulled into my parking spot. As we got out of the vehicle and walked the half block to our apartment I noticed a small cat gently trailing behind us. As we turned the corner there were several doors, one for each apartment. The black cat passed by us and went up to the very door of our apartment as if she already knew exactly where her home was.

The cat's right paw was lifted similar to a dog getting ready to shake someone's hand and when I opened the door the cat sat on her haunches and peered into the dark room. She would look at me and then into the condo back and forth. I softly said, "if you go into the room you will become my cat." She immediately went into the condo. We noticed she was hungry and very malnourished. It was obvious she was a stray living out in the desert. Kitty Kitty, as we began calling her, was very polite and already house-trained.

She began exhibiting traits very much like Daisy. I told my girlfriend that I thought Kitty Kitty was my childhood dog. Even though my girlfriend was open to past lives, she held some reservations. One day while we were both sitting on the couch, I switched off the television. I looked at Kitty Kitty who was sitting in front of the television watching us. I felt a nudge on the inner to ask her a question so I looked at Kitty Kitty and said, "Are you Daisy my dog?" She looked directly at us and very distinctly nodded her head full up and down three times as a human would say yes. We were both completely shocked. I have never seen her or any other animal make that gesture.

When we moved back to Virginia we shortened her name from Kitty Kitty to KiKi. Since that time she has continued to exhibit other qualities and characteristics of my dog, such as Daisy's love of water and dislike of collars. KiKi enjoyed baths and swimming, while she would find her way out of every collar much like Daisy. Daisy chewed through half a dozen collars the first year I had her until my mom and I gave up trying to put one on.

I remember a time when I moved two houses away and with every trip made to carry stuff to the new place, KiKi would follow me to the new house and then lead the way back to the old house much like Daisy. By now my girlfriend was convinced KiKi was my dog reincarnated.

During the next few years I would often go away for trips to Guidance for a Better Life. Every time I would return home KiKi would come up to say hello, then disappear for the same amount of time I had been gone, whether it was two days or over a week. I strongly suspected that this was a left over expression of how she felt when I left her when she was Daisy.

At Guidance for a Better Life I was taught many lessons about the beauty of reincarnation. We are Soul, and animals are Soul too. As Soul we are eternal beings made of God's Light and Sound and Love. If our love connection with another is strong we can be blessed to reincarnate to be together again. The joy of being reunited with this special companion has healed a deep spot in my childhood heart. I am still blessed to have her with me to this day and to continue our wonderful relationship.

Written by Thorin Blanco

19

Sweet Dreams

Singing HU and asking for a dream before falling asleep helps you tune in and raise up to receive and better remember the experience. Most importantly it is also a form of drawing nigh. Anyone seeking a closer relationship with the Divine should consider this sacred principle. When you draw nigh to God, God will respond.

"Sweet Dreams" with a smiley face was written on the white board by Del, my spiritual teacher at Guidance for a Better Life in Love, Virginia. It was one of the first retreats I had attended back in the 1990's. When I arrived that day I looked at the grassy dam that held back the waters from the pond and was excited to place my one-person backpacking tent as close to the water as possible.

As I crawled into my tent and made efforts to get comfortable in my sleeping bag I listened to the night sounds of bullfrogs, birds, and insects. The air seemed alive with sound. I was very excited and asked Divine Spirit to please bring me a dream that was in my best spiritual interest and help me remember the dream. Del had made those suggestions during the retreat with the option to share our dream experiences in class the next morning.

I sang HU, a pure prayer to God. In a moment I was aware of three spiritual beings kneeling on either side of me. They were made of white translucent light. Silently they wrapped me in what felt like a very soft, deep, downy comforter. The thin sleeping mat on which I was resting seemed to disappear. I was wrapped in this comforter as a child may be swaddled in a blanket of love by its father or mother. I felt the gentlest peace and love fill my being and was aware of being lifted up. The next morning I woke in the physical and felt well rested, refreshed, and happy with the memory of the amazing experience of being tucked in at bedtime as never before.

It seems remembering those moments when Soul was raised up in consciousness was more important than remembering the dreams that continued on through the night. The experience helped me grow in realization that I am Soul, a Divine spark of God. As Soul I can travel safely under the guidance of God's Prophet. I have learned that I am loved and given the experiences that are perfect for my spiritual unfoldment. God's timing is perfect.

Over time and daily practice of singing HU, I have come to know that the spiritual beings who nourished me with comfort and love are the Prophet and his co-workers. That experience showed me I am divinely guided and protected when traveling the vast inner worlds in the dream state. It is very reassuring to be in the presence of the one who knows the way, knows me, and knows my needs on my journey home to the Heart of God. Once you are touched by the Hand of God, it is not easily forgotten. The experience of God's Love is different from the experience of human love and cannot be measured or explained in words. The human standard of what I thought love to be has changed as my view of Divine Love grows through personal experiences with the Divine. With a sincere intent and prayer in your heart to experience Divine Love, it can happen. I am grateful for the outer and inner guidance available through the Prophet, the Comforter of our time.

Written by Ann Atwell

20

Prayed for a Friend

Our prayers are answered when it is in the best spiritual interest of everyone involved. Sometimes it is not merely enough to ask of God. We must "listen" and act on guidance received to help God make our prayers a reality. We play an active part and the timing can be important.

My husband and I homeschool our children, and one winter I was concerned that our eldest son did not have enough social interactions with boys his age. His playmate who had been coming to my home daycare had transitioned to kindergarten at the public school. While our son had several friends who are girls, I was concerned that he was missing having boys his age to play and wrestle with. So I took my concern to God and prayed. I prayed not only for him to have a friend, but also for myself to like the mom, so that I could have a new friend as well.

We had been planning on giving our kids swim lessons at the local YMCA, but I felt guided to do it sooner than we originally had thought. So I listened to that inner guidance and signed the kids up for classes. At the first lesson I noticed a mom walk in with two boys. I felt kind of shy but talked with her a little and felt comfortable with her right away. After a few classes of sitting on the bleachers with our youngest boys squirming and playing together with trucks, I felt like she was the answer to my prayer. So I asked to exchange phone numbers and we have been friends now for several years.

The thing that touches me most from this experience is that the prayer was answered above and beyond what I had asked for with my limited vision. God had not only given my eldest son and me great friends with similar interests, He also knew that we both had younger children that would get along great too.

A few weeks ago I shared with my friend that she was an answer to my prayer, at which point she shared that she too had been praying for a friend for herself and her boys. God is great! He answers our prayers even better than we can imagine, all because He loves us.

Written by Molly Comfort

21

Bay Leaves Bring Romantic Cabin for Two

Guidance from God can come in many ways and be about any part of our life. Sometimes it can be very obvious, sometimes very subtle. The key is being aware and learning to trust what your heart knows to be true, regardless of what anyone else says.

In the summer of 2013 my husband Mark and I were planning a weeklong vacation in Houghton Lake, Michigan to visit friends and family. We currently live in Virginia so all our searching had to be done on the internet. We found a listing "Romantic Cabin for Two" that looked promising, but it was twenty minutes away from my aunt's house. My aunt thought we should rent a cabin that was across the street from her. Which to pick? It was hard to decide if we should be closer to her or enjoy the nicer lake getaway. I asked my inner guide, the Prophet, for help and then went about the day.

While at the store shopping the next day I was cruising an isle of spices when a bag of bay leaves caught my eye. I picked it up and opened the twist tie to inhale the rich aroma of the leaves. They smelled wonderful. Even though I did not need them I threw them in the cart. Later that night I was looking at a map of Houghton Lake to see exactly where the cabin we liked was in relation to my aunt's house. I discovered it was located on the bay. Then I realized my strong attraction to the bay leaves was telling me to stick with my original choice, the cabin on the bay!

I shared this awake dream during my first Dream Retreat at Guidance for a Better Life and the teacher, Del IV, helped me see a pearl of wisdom in this experience. He asked the question, "What if the bay leaves meant to leave the bay?" (Bay- LEAVE). I took a moment to check how I felt. He told me not to change my answer. He reminded me to follow my heart when interpreting an awake dream. Awake dreams most often are confirmations of what we already know to be true.

Mark and I decided to book the romantic

cabin. I attended the Dream Retreat before I went on vacation so this was a good opportunity to test my "truth detector." This is something I learned about at Guidance for a Better Life. We all have one; it is a blessing from God that helps me to navigate through life. It allows me to know truth when I hear it and has been strengthened as I have learned to trust my inner communication from the Prophet.

Sure enough, when Mark and I pulled up the gravel drive to the bayside cabin our jaws were dropping. The entire place inside and out was put together with so much love. It was more beautiful than the pictures online. Even my aunt, who was originally disappointed in our decision, said we made the right choice.

God can use anything, even a bay leaf, to get a message across if we are receptive to Its Voice. We can ask God for help. There is no issue too small. If it is important to us, it is important to God. We are Soul and as such God has given us the ability to receive Its guidance. This inner communication is my lifeline. Knowing that God is still active and guiding me has made my life such a joy to live. We are never alone!

Written by Carmen Snodgrass

22

My Comfort Zone and the Pond

Fear is a condenser. It restricts our ability to follow our heart and ultimately accept God's Love. Life becomes an ever smaller box in which we hide from the possibility of failure or being hurt. If you want to live a truly abundant life do what it takes to move past your fears.

During a retreat at Guidance for a Better Life in November 2013 it was abundantly shown to me how I was living within a comfort zone, addicted to creature comfort. This comfort zone was created by my own brain, mostly out of fear. There was nothing rational about it. During the retreat my teacher was given an insight that as a group, we needed to go into the cold pond, completely clothed. I was mostly excited for this and knew it would somehow be good for me.

Into the pond we went completely clothed in our jeans and t-shirts. We enthusiastically followed our teacher in, one hundred percent. We all trusted and knew it was in our best interest, as silly as it may have seemed at the time. When I got out of the pond I felt exhilarated, activated, and ALIVE! After getting out of the pond, I remembered how much I enjoyed going into that cold pond as a child.

This reawakened dreams in me that were squashed down by my brain, because pursuing those dreams meant stretching and growing beyond my comfort zone. I had been yearning to move out on my own to a different city, get married, have kids, and live life more fully, among many other things. All of these things hold some risk and lots of change, both of which can be uncomfortable. I knew moving out was in my best interest, but I allowed the fear of failure and fear of being outside my comfort zone, to weigh me down.

The funny thing about fear is that it may seem small and insignificant at first, but as you give in to it, over time fear can grow stronger and stronger. As it grew stronger I allowed it to control me and then the comfort zone I lived in grew smaller. Once I made the decision that I was going to stretch my comfort zone, life was exciting again. I made myself do things that I had thought of doing in the past, but never really got around to. I asked my inner guide, the Prophet, for help completing these. After each successful completion, my confidence grew and the fear lessened.

Now I have started a new job in a new city. I bought a house, live on my own, and I am engaged to be married. The satisfaction I get out of being able to pay my own bills, budget my money, and take care of myself and a pet is far more rewarding than I ever dreamed it could be.

Written by Michelle K. Reuschling

23

Thank You Betty Jo

A good marriage is based on love for God and love for each other. It should also help us grow in our ability to serve by inspiring us to "think of others." In the following story a loving mother makes the brave choice to live longer as a gift. A gift that will help her son and daughter-in-law's marriage grow in both love and service.

I am so very blessed to be married to a wonderful, loving husband. Paul and I have been married almost twelve years. Our relationship has always been loving and peaceful. It is built on our love and respect for each other, and on our love for God who is the foundation of our relationship and marriage. We are blessed to be on similar spiritual paths. We both regularly attend retreats at Guidance for a Better Life led by Del Hall, a true Prophet of God. Last year in a class at the retreat center the Holy Spirit, through Del, lovingly made me aware that as good as Paul's and my marriage was, there was a lot of room for growth for us both. It had the potential to be so much better.

Living single for much of my adult life and marrying Paul later in life I had selfish tendencies and brought those into our marriage. Because I lived single for so long I did not trust that our marriage would last. This attitude put a wedge between us that I was not aware of. For the most part we lived like roommates, keeping our finances separate and even doing our own laundry. By keeping things separate we both had an "out" should our marriage not succeed.

Still, we loved each other and knew we were very blessed. In addition to being blessed with a wonderful husband, I am blessed to have had the most wonderful mother-in-law. From the beginning of Paul's and my friendship his mom Betty Jo accepted and embraced me with open arms and an open heart. She treated me with love, warmth, and respect. She was a kind hearted, loving, funny lady, and a committed Christian who loved Jesus with all of her heart. Over the years I grew to love her deeply.

In 2009 Betty Jo was diagnosed with dementia. She eventually moved to a independent living apartment about a mile from our home. Paul was her main caretaker as her other three sons lived out of the area. Paul and I spent a lot of cherished time with her. Almost every Sunday afternoon we would eat lunch or dinner together and then play a fun game of Scrabble. My love for her grew.

In November of 2014, at the age of eighty-eight, Betty Jo was diagnosed with a rare form of cancer. The prognosis was a life expectancy of a few years maximum. When Paul gently told her of the diagnosis she reacted to the news with amazing joy and trust in the Lord. She knew she was going to Heaven when she passed, and that she would once again see her mother and dad, husband, and two brothers.

Daily radiation on weekdays, and once-a-week chemotherapy treatments began immediately. Paul took her to treatments most days. I felt a deep desire in my heart to help Paul and Betty Jo by taking her to a radiation treatment once a week. My prayers were answered by the Prophet, who knowing my heart's desire cleared the way for me to take time off from work each week during the busiest time of the year at my job, the Christmas holidays. During this precious time with Betty Jo my heart expanded with love, as I grew to love her even more. I felt so close to her. A special loving bond grew between us.

Toward the end of December the radiation and chemotherapy treatments were curtailed. Her doctors determined that the treatments were not helping her and were causing her painful side effects and making her very weak. Her doctors diagnosed that the cancer was advancing and said she had only days to a few weeks to live.

Paul found a nursing home located within a mile of our home. He visited his mom almost every day and I visited her several times a week. After a couple of weeks Betty Jo's health actually started to improve. She got her appetite back and starting gaining strength. We were amazed at her progress. It was truly a miracle of God! I treasured the time we spent together. It was a blessing for me to visit her and spend time with her, and do what I could to help her. We shared many precious moments. I was also helping Paul by taking care of things at our home while he was with his mom. My love for him grew too, and our marriage grew stronger during this difficult yet blessed time. At the beginning of March, Paul was able to have Betty Jo moved to an assisted living home, which was much better suited for her needs. Now, her health once again began to decline. We knew it was a matter of time.

During a weekend retreat at Guidance for a Better Life in March, Paul and I shared with Del the latest on Betty Jo's condition and that she had amazingly outlived her prognosis by several months. Del lovingly provided insight to us that as Soul, on the inner, Betty Jo had been given the choice to pass away and leave her body shortly after her cancer diagnosis, or stay alive in her body longer so that I could grow by serving her and serving Paul and Paul and I could grow closer in our marriage. Out of her deep love for both of us she chose to stay in her failing body, enduring treatments, pain, and declining health. What an amazing beautiful gift of love Betty Jo gave me – and Paul! I knew that Del was right. I reflected on how she looks at me sometimes, eye to eye, conveying so much love and caring in a look, no words spoken between us. It all made so much sense and felt right. I can not begin to describe the love and gratitude I felt at that moment for Betty Jo and for her choosing to stay on to help Paul and me. It was all about love. Serving others with love and God is such a blessing to others. What is amazing is that I am so blessed while serving!

That same weekend Del led the group in singing HU together for twenty minutes. During the quiet time afterward I prayed to please let Betty Jo know on the inner how much I love her and how grateful I am to her for agreeing to stay alive longer in her body to give me the opportunity to grow in my love for and service to others. The Prophet then gave me the gift of seeing Betty Jo on the inner so that I could thank her! She was beautiful, a radiant light body, standing tall in perfect health, dressed in white with golden light all around her. We hugged. I expressed to her how much I love her and am so grateful to her for agreeing to stay alive longer in her body to help me grow, and to help Paul and I grow in our marriage, and what a beautiful gift of love she gave. Smiling beautifully with love in her eyes she expressed to me she loves me too, very much.

By her staying longer in the body, the Prophet with her and through her taught me what unselfish love and true service to others mean. Ten days later, on April 1, Betty Jo as Soul left her failing body. I felt relief – for her. I feel a deep love and appreciation for her that I just cannot put into words, and which continue to grow. My love and appreciation for Paul continues to grow. We both have grown in our love for and service to each other. Our marriage is being healed by the Prophet, who knows us better than we know ourselves. He knows what we need to live an abundant life of love and service to one-another. That's what he desires for all of us – to have a full and abundant life.

Written by Cathy Sandman

24

I Am Soul, Light and Sound of God

There are certain "Core Truths" we teach at our retreats. Not only are they taught, folks actually get to experience them. One of the most important of these truths is "You do not have a Soul" rather, "You are Soul." This seemingly simple switch in perspective can set you free.

Many years ago, my father and spiritual teacher, the Prophet, shared a simple yet profound Divine truth with me and a class of students at Guidance for a Better Life. He shared with the group that we are Soul that has a body. Not what we had commonly thought - that we are a human body that has a Soul. He went on to give an example that it would be like identifying with ourselves as our cars - not as the driver, the animator, on the inside. Our "cars" will wear out over time but the real "us" will carry on and can get new "cars" for the next leg of our spiritual journey.

This simple, yet profound truth lifted a veil of illusion and opened the doors for so many wonderful possibilities and opportunities. Hearing and knowing that we are Soul meant that we are eternal. We are a Divine spark of God. We are children of God, created out of the Light and Sound of God and our potential for spiritual freedom, growth, and love is infinite.

Our bodies are a gift from God, to be respected and cared for, but it is not who we are, nor does it limit our connection with the Divine. As Soul we can be taught by an inner and outer spiritual guide. Together with our guide we are free to explore God's amazing inner worlds, the various Heavens, in dreams and contemplations.

In one such contemplation, after singing HU, I found myself as Soul with my spiritual guide on an inner plane. We were on the beach at a vast and beautiful ocean. The golden light from the sun was shining down on us - it was warm and comforting. It bathed us in waves of love, peace, joy, security, and more. It was the Divine Light of God. The freedom and boundlessness of experiencing a moment purely as Soul is something that was never possible in my human body. I was able to feel absolute stillness and activity all at once and an indescribable strength in experiencing the real me. I felt free from the weight of the world and loved by God beyond my wildest imagination.

Our true home as Soul is the Heart of God. Thinking about that reality consciously reminds me who I really am at my core and brings with it so much peace. I may have a challenging day at work but knowing that I am Soul and not alone keeps a "bigger picture" and the "eternal view" present in my mind and heart. The events in daily life are less able to consume me when kept in perspective. As Soul I know that God has prepared me with everything I will ever need for my spiritual journey.

When I heard my father say, "I am Soul" I knew what I was hearing was truth. Over many years and through many experiences the truth revealed that night has sunk in deeper and deeper. The Divine has blessed me with personal experiences that solidified the knowingness in my heart. Even still, I know there is so much more to discover regarding the truth that we are Soul.

Written by Catherine Hughes

25

The Divine Led Me to School

When you stop rushing through life and make the conscious choice to seek a deeper relationship with God, you will receive help to take the next step. In this story two inner spiritual guides, sent by God, led the seeker to her next step. She found the missing "peace" that she wanted. Pray to be led in the direction that is right for you.

I always knew there was a God and that He must be working in my life, but felt somehow there had to be more to this relationship. I did not understand our relationship and felt disconnected from Him. For quite a while I went through a time of seeking answers to my questions about God and what were His true teachings. So I went to different churches and organizations trying to find answers. I felt like so many pieces were missing in my life and my relationship with God.

For several years my husband had been attending spiritual retreats at Guidance for a Better Life and it was clear that was right for him. I signed up for a couple of retreats and enjoyed it, but was still looking for confirmation on what direction was right for me. I did not want to simply follow my husband, but to know it was the right decision for me. One day during my search I attended a spiritual seminar in Pennsylvania. I had that question about the right path for me in my mind and heart the day of the seminar. Life was busy with a four-month-old baby and a new job starting soon, and I also wanted to know how I could have more balance in my life.

I closed my eyes and with a grateful heart sang HU, a love song to God. Quickly I saw myself as Soul sitting in Virginia at the Guidance for a Better Life retreat center near the pond. I was so very calm and thoroughly enjoying the surroundings. My attention was drawn to a path going up a hill and I realized two spiritual guides were there pointing out a dirt road and then leading me toward it. The road felt so familiar and important, like we had walked together in the past. I had been looking for this path. The two guides and I looked down noticing a small creek that seemed more like a large river rushing with waves of water. It reminded me of Spirit flowing to everything around it, like this was the source of Divine blessings. I saw rocks in different places, but the water was rolling right over them so beautifully. It made me think about how there are obstacles in life, but you can go gracefully through them when walking with Divine guidance.

One of the guides walked up and gave me a gift that was wrapped with a blue ribbon. It was a ball of light. I knew it was a reminder of my true nature as Soul, a Divine spark of God. The gift reminded me that as Soul I do have balance. The guides also gave me a message. It was to "Walk in Balance and Harmony." With that message I felt great peace and reassurance within me. I knew and recognized this phrase from Del at Guidance for a Better Life. This was the inner confirmation I had been seeking. Spirit was showing me what was in my heart, that Guidance for a Better Life was the right place for me to learn God's ways.

This very real experience gave me confidence to know that I was following my heart and knew where to find what I needed. It was a turning point for me to recognize and trust what I was receiving. It was not my mind but my true self, Soul, that heard the Divine guidance. I am thankful every day that I listened to that Divine communication and followed through to continue attending retreats at the retreat center. I have experienced so much of God's truth and been given so many spiritual tools over the years. I no longer feel like there is a missing piece in my relationship with God. I cherish that I have a loving and personal connection with God and His Prophet. I appreciate the guidance in my life. I know that the Divine has a perfect plan for my life, and I love watching it develop with His guidance.

Written by Michelle Hibshman

26

Is Your Dog Like Ours?

What is it that keeps some from accepting the loving hand that has been offered? When will we realize our potential and begin to truly be free? Why do we run our lives in circles versus taking a more direct route home to God?

We recently adopted a rescued dog. She is about four years old with an uncertain history. It is apparent that she has had less than an ideal life. She can be very timid, lack self-confidence, and "startles" at unexpected events. We have been very patient with her, showing her much love and attention. Very slowly she is coming out of her "shell" and reacting positively to the love being offered.

Despite our best efforts there are still times she baffles us. We have never raised a hand to her, but as is the case with many dogs like this, she may flinch if we move too fast. We may go to show her affection and love, and she might withdraw and move away. At these times we may call her or attempt to move closer, but with every step we take to close the gap she may take one, two, or more steps away. As a Labrador Retriever she is bred for the water, but hiking through the woods revealed that she has never encountered small creeks or bodies of water. Despite wanting desperately to follow us, her uncertainty about something new, such as wading through shallow water, keeps her from taking the most direct path. She runs up and down the creek looking for narrow places where she may jump across without getting her feet wet.

Then there are the times when her fear and uncertainty disappear and she becomes the dog she was born to be. We see her full of joy as she runs around the yard playing with other dogs. Her potential emerges as she sets off running with abandon on a forest trail happy as any dog could be. We see the love in her as she turns and gallops full speed back to us after a whistle call. In these times we see her true self. Observing these inherent qualities manifest in her as she begins operating in the world as her true self opens our hearts, and we work to develop those qualities.

My heart opens with joy as I see her take

those first tentative steps into the creek, crossing that unknown as quickly as she can. This leads to wading confidently up and down the creek and eventually to swimming as she explores new adventures. Noticing that she loves to follow deer tracks through the woods, we are working with her inborn scenting ability to follow tracks. Her anticipation and excitement grow as one of us will hold her as the other takes off running through the woods. Hiding hundreds of yards away over hills and behind trees is no deterrent as she follows the scent confidently and methodically. She will stay on track until we are discovered. We all react with joy at these reunions.

This four-legged creature is constantly reminding me of how we humans act in our relationship with the Divine. God loves us so very much, more than we could ever fully understand. God sees our full potential and knows intimately what we could become. God knows us better than we know ourselves and has His Hand out in love; His voice has been calling us home for a very long time. Our true nature is Soul. Soul is a Divine spark of God, created by God to express the Divine qualities that are inherent in us. We were created to experience and express truth, love, joy, and peace. The Divine qualities of wisdom and clarity are part of our true nature.

We hear God's Voice calling us, but fear, uncertainty, or other distractions, keep us from drawing closer to God. When God reaches out a hand of love do we eagerly run toward the source to experience all that is being offered or do we hold back for some long forgotten reason? Instead of taking the direct path to God, do we act like our dog who runs up and down the bank of the stream looking for what we might consider to be a better way, resisting what is right before us?

God knows our true self better than we do. God hears every true prayer of our heart and has an open hand offering those Divine qualities that we know is in our heart of hearts. If we can see the potential in our pets and want to nurture and develop what is best for them, think how much more God can see in us and wants for us. At Guidance for a Better Life our teacher, a true Prophet of God, teaches us to listen to that still small voice inside. We learn to draw close to God, to take hold of and accept His outstretched hand, and to stay on track and follow the direct path home to God.

Written by Paul Nelson

27

I Feel Right With God

Dreams are so much more than simply images. They are not just a television set on the back of our eyelids projected by the mind that we passively watch. They are memories of our active experiences in the greater worlds of Spirit and one way that God can teach and bless us. Sometimes a dream might contain a profound truth but leave no visual memory but rather, a knowingness. Do not discount these.

It was early March and I could hear the cold biting wind outside nipping at the windows of the log cabin we were staying in. I was in that cozy place between the dream world and the world where my physical body lay resting. I tried to gently go over my dream so I could record it in my dream journal. Eyes still closed, I continued to stay in that space, savoring it. No images of the adventures I had drifted into my consciousness, just a feeling. A deep solid as a rock, sink-your-teeth-into kind of feeling. As I rubbed the sleep from my eyes and pulled my dream journal closer to write, I lay there stumped. I had no words to write. I could not remember any details of the experience I had just left.

Journaling my dreams is one way I demonstrate gratitude for the sacred experiences I have been given, so pulling my pen cap off I began to write. "I don't remember my dream, but I woke up feeling right with God." I climbed down the ladder to the main cabin area and after a warm breakfast of home cooked oatmeal we gathered at the table for class. We began our small class by sharing our dreams from the night before with our teacher Del Hall.

Soon it was my opportunity to share. I felt a little sheepish thinking I did not have much to share with the group. Del listened with full attention as I shared not remembering my dream but waking up and feeling right with God. Del's eyes smiled as he said, "one of the most important aspects of a dream is what God is trying to communicate to us." He continued, "most people would love to wake up feeling right with God." I sat there jaw slightly dropped. "I feel right with God." The gravity and magnitude of those seemingly simple words slowly sunk in. My heart overflowed with love. I was immediately glad I had spoken up and shared my dream, and even more grateful to Del for personally helping me to understand the gift of love I had been given.

To this day I cherish that dream. I often revisit that moment where I remember being snuggled warm in my sleeping bag and nestled in God's Heart. That feeling so lovingly placed in my heart continues to bless me and provide me with spiritual nourishment, bringing me comfort and strength when the storms in life make the surface waves choppy and I seek something solid under my feet.

Back in the cabin at Guidance for a Better Life Del's discourse on dreams continued as we learned how to become more fluent in the language of the Divine, to better understand the subtle inner communication we all have. Del taught us many things that morning such as sometimes all we remember when we wake is a sound or a color. At other times we wake with just a feeling or a knowing that a personal message from God was placed directly in our hearts. I felt a week's worth of learning and truth was imparted into our hearts in the following hours, and before we could blink it was time for lunch.

Sitting around that table, warmed by the steadily burning fire in the wood stove and the truth in Del's words, I learned the importance of trusting my experiences. I learned the importance of having a teacher to personally help me understand the blessings I have been given. Especially when it is a "simple dream," like waking up feeling right with God.

Written by Ahna Spitale

28

Door is Opened to Freedom

In a very real sense many people on Earth live in a prison. A prison of consciousness. It is here we are blinded to the divinity within us. It is here we are trapped by the illusion that there is nothing more. It is here we get so wrapped up with the non-stop distractions, that even if the prison door was open, some would not know to step through it. Fortunately, some do.

I was in my thirties and was experiencing an inner unrest. I did not know or understand at the time what it was but there was something deep within me stirring. I did not know what this unrest was or how to resolve it. I was seeking something, but what? I had a beautiful family, friends, home, and wonderful comforts but something was calling to me. One night the desperate feeling was so intense I called out in a prayer "I want to go home." It surprised me, I did not know what this meant but it came from a deep place within me.

I received a brochure for Guidance for a Better Life in the mail a short time after that experience. After some consideration I decided to go and it changed my life in so many good ways. I am blessed with a spiritual teacher that has given me spiritual tools and over time changed the unrest to peace within me. One of the tools given was the study of dreams.

I had a dream that seemed simple but defined me and my journey in life prior to going to the retreat center. In this dream I was in a clean, tidy, comfortable, and nicely decorated room. I looked around and it became apparent that the room was a prison cell. The cell door was open and on the other side were my spiritual teacher, the Prophet, and two other teachers. I was being given the opportunity to get out of the prison cell.

At the time I did not recognize I was living my life as if living in a prison cell. My life from all outward appearance was well, yet something inside me knew differently. The prison cell represented things that limited my freedom; fears, worries, vanity, attachments, negative attitudes, as well as unhealed experiences from past lives. I did not realize I was living in a prison cell because it was comfortable and familiar.

In the dream I hesitated to leave the confinement of the cell. I seemed to be frozen in my old familiar ways. When the door started to close I made the decision to leave the confines of the cell and took full hold of my spiritual teacher. Through the years he has been teaching me and giving me spiritual tools to use to break free of the prison of human consciousness. The Prophet opened a doorway to a new way of living where I now experience love, joy, peace, and a freedom I have never known.

Written by Renée Dinwiddie

29

After Twenty-Eight Years
I Know

You are so much more than your physical body. You are Soul, an eternal spiritual being created from God's Light. In essence, you are a piece of the Holy Ghost and have similar attributes. This might be hard for some to believe or accept but nonetheless it is true. If it is your desire to experience this truth for yourself, it is possible.

About twenty-eight years ago I was given a gift from a relative at Christmas. It was a cassette tape series by a minister called Reincarnation, Karma, and Resurrection. After listening to it I easily accepted the ideas presented on the tapes. These tapes whet my appetite for more spiritual information, which also led me to changing my diet, which by the way was in serious need of change since I was not physically feeling well. That same New Years I made a resolution to change my diet to an all natural diet free from sugar and white flour products. After loosing thirty-five pounds in three months I felt much calmer. After all the spiritual reading and diet changes I finally decided to sit and pray. I decided to try some of the spiritual exercises that I had been reading about.

I came home after working late one night, sat on the couch, and closed my eyes. I began to focus my attention at the spot between my eyes slightly above the eyebrows called the spiritual eye. I began to breathe deeply and became more relaxed with each breath. I suddenly found myself floating in a dark void feeling extremely calm when a pin-sized light appeared in what seemed like a distance away. As I focused on this light it began to grow and came closer and closer to me all the while I was caught up in the experiencing of God's Love. I had a sense that it was the Light of God, but I was not sure since I had no reference point. What I know is that I was so excited that all I could think at that moment was that I wanted to go into that light or get even closer to it. Something or someone was holding me in my body not allowing me to go. I became a little frustrated that I could not go and the experience subsided until I came back to full body consciousness.

After that experience I began to read two to three books a week trying to figure out what had just happened. Several years had passed and after much study, praying, and contemplating I think I ended up with a case of spiritual indigestion and found myself in a dead zone, so to speak. Thankfully a friend of mine sent me a brochure for Guidance for a Better Life in Virginia and I decided to take a weeklong retreat during the summer of 2006. Del introduced me to many new ideas and tools for spiritual growth, one of which was HU. I learned HU is a love song to God and an ancient name for God. On a more technical note, HU is a vibration and when sung for a short time can help tune us to become more receptive to Divine guidance. My spiritual coals, which were almost out, had now become reignited.

In the summer of 2014, at a weeklong retreat, I was blessed with an experience with the Light and Sound of God. This experience helped me to understand on a deeper level my first experience with the Light of God twenty-eight years ago. Del, the Prophet of God, led the group in an exercise in the Light and Sound of God. As we sang "I am Light and Sound" I became lighter and lighter until I saw with my inner vision God's Light as far as the eye could see. I was invited into this light. Light was everywhere and then I got a nudge to look down and saw myself as light. I looked just like the light that surrounded me. I was made of the same stuff. Yet I was aware that I was me too, an individualized spark of the Light of God, made of the essence of God. It took twenty-eight years. That is how long I needed to be made ready to accept the blessing of realizing that I am Soul, an individualized spark of the Light of God.

Written by Sam Spitale

30

Love Thyself

You are here on Earth to become more refined in your ability to give and receive love. Of the two, more seem to struggle with receiving, especially when it is from our self. Regardless of how you "feel," the fact remains — you are worthy.

When I first came to Guidance for a Better Life I was shy and self-conscious, full of anxiety and guilt, carrying a sadness around with me as my own. I felt unworthy of God's Love based on a false mental view of myself. It took many experiences to break through this, to realize I was looking at myself from my mind, instead of viewing myself as Soul, my spiritual side, my true self. Slowly, I quit beating myself up as much and began accepting that I am worthy of God's Love. I am not the mistakes I blew all out of proportion. I learned to forgive and love myself.

An inner experience at Guidance for a Better Life, during a spiritual exercise, helped me to see this truth more clearly. Del, the Prophet, took me on a journey to a Temple of God. It was beautiful beyond description and filled with God's Love. In the center, a beam of Light was shining on an open book on a pedestal, God's Book. The Prophet encouraged me to read from it. I stepped into the beam and read "Love Thyself with all Thy Heart and Soul."

I knew I could no longer beat myself up, or judge myself so harshly. I also realized that I could not truly love God until I could love It's creation, me, Soul, a particle of It's Holy Spirit. This is helping me accept a profound truth, "Soul exists because God loves It." My existence, every breath, every moment of life, is a gift from God to be cherished.

I am grateful to the Prophet for being with me every step of the way on my journey of growth and discovery, for his guidance, protection, and truth. It is by accepting Prophet's hand, and the relationship that followed, that has allowed me to move from a limited and miserable view of myself to the boundless one of Soul. Surrendering my old ways of thinking, many based on half-truths and falsehoods, gives me the freedom to pursue a life of abundance.

Written by Gary Caudle

31

The Blue Light of God

The Light of God manifests itself in many different colors. Each color has a specific meaning and can provide additional insight into the nature of your experience. To witness any aspect of the Light of God is a profound blessing and an expression of God's Love for you.

Before I attended my first retreat at Guidance for a Better Life I had come across references to spiritual light in books and heard people talk about it, but this light was nonetheless a mental concept to me. It was something that I had no personal experience with. All of this changed during my first retreat at the retreat center. I was sitting out in the woods one evening as part of an awareness exercise when a beautiful deer walked in front of me. It was alerted by a slight turn of my head and started snorting and moving its head back and forth as it tried to identify me amid the fading light of day. My heart went out to the deer, as I felt love for this part of God's creation, when suddenly everything in my field of vision - the deer, the trees, everything around me - became filled with a shimmering blue light. During this I felt Divine Love flood into my heart and fill my whole being.

The deer then bounded off and I stood up, amazed by what had just taken place. I had the knowing in my heart that Divine Spirit is real, and that what I had just experienced was way beyond anything that I could ever perceive with my physical senses alone. When I shared this experience with Del he did not seem at all surprised. He said that it was great and an important step on my path, and that there is a lot of spiritual help available to me. This experience was so stunning to me that I felt compelled to return to the retreat center for a spiritual retreat and learn more about this amazing blue light.

As I attended more retreats and continued to have more experiences with the blue light, both on and off of the retreat center property, in dreams and while awake, I came to learn that this light was one of the aspects of the Light of God. It was also the calling card of my inner spiritual guide and teacher, the one who is a true Prophet of God. This beautiful blue light has been a constant companion to me over the twenty years that have passed since that unforgettable summer evening at Guidance for a Better Life.

Sometimes it comes as a flash of light so small that I could easily miss it if I was not paying attention. Whenever I see it, it is a welcome reminder that my guide and teacher is spiritually with me. This presence helps me to make better choices that have led to a life of an abundance of peace, love, and the strength to endure life's challenges. This is an abundance that I never dreamed was possible twenty years ago when all that I could see was filled with the blue Light of God. I am grateful to Del and Guidance for a Better Life for creating a peaceful, relaxed setting, away from the stresses of daily life in which to experience God's Love and Its Light, a light that has within it everything that I need.

Written by Roland Vonder Muhll

32

Past Life Connection

There is a reason you are naturally drawn to, or turned off by, certain people the first time you meet. It is because those you come to know on your journey through time can appear again and again in your many lives. Your mind may not have the memory of the connection, but Soul does. God can bring you back together as a gift to continue in your shared growth.

A friend from work invited me to share lunch with her recently. We went to the cafeteria and enjoyed sharing a meal during our busy day. She suggested we share something about ourselves that interests us, something we have not yet discussed. Given we are relatively new friends that was easy. I spoke about my love for medicinal plants and the use of some to make lip balm. Recently I had taught a five-year-old friend how to make lip balm. It was so much fun to share this simple skill. During our lunch conversation I remembered learning the process at a Plant Walk class in the Pocono Mountains, the weekend of September 7, 1994. It was the same weekend I met Del and Lynne Hall who teach at Guidance for a Better Life here in Virginia.

My friend shared of her love to make prayer beads. Her love for making them began years ago when she was living in California. A book fell off a shelf in a store and landed in her hands. It was titled "A String and A Prayer." She literally slept with the book for days afterwards. "It was like finding an old friend." She feels Divine Spirit uses her to create prayer beads for others. As the conversation continued she shared a past life memory as a Native American. In that lifetime she made beaded Medicine Shields for others.

I was delighted to learn she believed in past lives. She asked if I had any past life recall. I recalled images from several dreams as a Native American and shared them with her. As she shared and I listened to her story, the words disappeared and her blue eyes began to change before me. I was looking deep into the eyes of an old friend. Tears welled up in my eyes and holy bumps covered my entire body for quite a while. I could barely speak. This Soul I knew and loved in a past life had re-entered my life in this moment of knowing. I felt joy, relief, comfort, and strength from this realization. My friend completely understood my response. Lunch now finished, we rode the elevator back down to work. I spontaneously said to my friend, "welcome home." We hugged and she now refers to me as her "old friend."

I have learned through experience at the Guidance for a Better Life retreat center that past lives are real and that I have had plenty of them. All of those experiences have helped me grow in the awareness that I am Soul, a Divine spark of God. Learning about past life connections has brought understanding from the past and healing that has helped free me in this lifetime. This spiritual freedom is granted from God through a relationship with His Prophet. This relationship is the key to finding spiritual freedom in this lifetime.

It is not always necessary to know past lives as this lifetime is filled with an abundance of goodness and love without looking back. Yet how grateful and blessed I am to meet once again an "old friend" while sharing lunch. How blessed I am that my spiritual guide found me in 1994 on a weekend Plant Walk in the mountains of Pennsylvania. He is my eternal teacher who connects the past with the present, allowing such blessings of helping old friends rekindle friendships. He taught me the HU song, a love song to God, which I was privileged to share with my "old friend."

Written by Ann Atwell

33

Guided to My Chiropractor

God can bless every area of our life. Nothing is "too small" to receive help with. The following is one such example of daily guidance from the Divine.

I woke up one morning with lower back pain and wanted to go to my chiropractor to get an adjustment. I thought, "It's Monday, he'll probably be too busy today." And so I dismissed getting the adjustment I needed.

I proceeded with my morning routine and then drove the kids to school. After taking the kids to school I drove back home. I got out of the car and headed toward the house when I noticed a business/calling card on the gravel in the driveway. I picked it up and adjusted the faded card so I could read it. It was the chiropractor's business card!

I knew this was Divine Spirit's way of communicating with me! So I listened to this message and proceeded to go to the chiropractor that same morning. He adjusted my back and I continue to feel great! The chance of finding his card right in my path (in my line of vision) was more than a coincidence... It was a gift from God. God cares about my well-being and sent me the encouragement to get the help I needed. I am very grateful.

Written by Moira Cervone

34

The Best Christmas Gift

*If someone offered you the opportunity to have your
own direct experiences with the Holy Ghost, to feel
God's Love personally, to gain wisdom on the
mysteries of life, bring more love and balance into your
life, and nurture a deeper relationship with the Divine
— would you accept it? If so, here is your chance.*

The best Christmas gift I ever got came the
week before Christmas, 2004. It was December
17, a day that would change my life forever.

The gift was not a new possession. It was not
something that could be bought or sold in any
store. The gift was this: a trusted friend taught
me to sing HU, a sacred love song to God. HU is
an ancient name for God that can be sung
quietly or aloud in prayer. HU has existed from
the beginning of time in one form or another
and is available to all regardless of religious
path. It is a pure way to express your love to
God and give thanks for your blessings.

When he shared HU with me I could feel that it was something very special. We sang HU together and I saw the Light of God for the first time. It was like nothing I had ever experienced before. It was more than just light; it brought a message of joy, clarity, peace, and most of all, that we are loved and not alone. Even though I had gone to church often as a child, this was the first time that I actually felt connected to the Holy Spirit. I have come to know that Jesus and all of his disciples sang HU. Singing HU conditions you to receive God's Love, and as we are able to receive more of God's Love, our lives become blessed with abundance (John 10:10).

After sharing HU my friend gave me a brochure for Guidance for a Better Life where he had learned about HU fifteen years before. I signed up for the first retreat that I was eligible for and my life has never been the same. Looking back to that December day in 2004, I had no idea the amazing journey that lay ahead. All I can say is that God is real, God loves you, and His mighty Hand reaches out to you.

Written by David Hughes

35

Lightning Storm of God's Love

The Light of God can manifest itself here in the physical in many ways. This expression of God's Love for us can appear in both the waking and sleeping states. Experiencing the Light of God in any form is a profound blessing and it can bring great comfort.

I had been traveling from my home state of Michigan to attend retreats at Guidance for a Better Life several times per year. The Prophet of God, Del Hall, who was my instructor at the retreat center; was also, by the Grace of God, my inner guide when I went back home and could not be in his physical presence in Virginia. I began to experience a life of hope, inner peace, and possibilities, which seemed to flourish in exponential proportions as I learned to include the Prophet in every facet of my existence.

There had been several significant changes in my life since I met and began studying under the tutelage of Del in the summer of 2006. Each event built on the one before as the Prophet lovingly helped me to see and know, through inner promptings, which decisions would be in my best interest at the time. One example of such guidance came in 2007 when my employer of ten years went bankrupt. I was, through a series of events, guided to apply for a job in a newly built manufacturing facility in a nearby town. The opportunity was incredible since not only had the slowing of the economy created a great deal of competition among job seekers, but this newly built state of the art facility was air conditioned and the benefits were superb. In February of 2008 after several interviews, I got the job.

I owned a manufactured home and by following the inner guidance from the Prophet, I was led to inquire with the management at the local manufactured home community. To my amazement, not only did they have a vacant home site, they were paying the cost of relocating the home! My home was moved to a location three minutes from my new place of employment.

The more my focus changed from my outer reality to my inner world, I began to have more clarity of purpose and the determination to grow and stretch towards living and being more of what I knew in my heart was possible. In order to do so, first, it became clear that it was necessary to let go of an attachment to a relationship that I was holding on to out of fear of loneliness. I needed to be released from the self made prison of staying in a situation that just did not work and as I invited the Prophet into this area, I have been given confidence that God's Love sustains me through all circumstances.

Shortly after moving into my home and putting an end to the aforementioned relationship, I had an experience that was quite out of the ordinary. I settled into what I thought was sleep. I looked out of the window and saw the most awe-inspiring lightning storm that I had ever witnessed. Strangely to me there was no sound; just rolling lightning that bolted and traveled continuously across the sky. Not only was the light captivating and beautiful, it offered a profound consolation that touched me at my core. The experience went on throughout the entire night and when I contemplated upon it, I came to the realization that I was offered comfort through the Light of God that was delivered to me in a way that would not frighten me. In time, as I grew in understanding, I realized that I actually enjoyed my own company and was not as lonely as I had feared I would be. A healing began that night which has and still is helping me to live a life more free from attachments to non-productive behaviors that had previously plagued my daily existence. It is a spiritual gift that stays in my heart to be remembered and treasured. It has personal value beyond measure.

I have had the privilege of continuing my spiritual studies with the Prophet's presence to guide and assist me in understanding that what I experienced that night was a particular manifestation of the Light of God. The lightning storm was not physical; it was God's healing spiritual Light given to me in a form that I was able to accept early in my journey. The gift of love and comfort was given to me at the time and in the way I needed it.

My faith is strengthened and I am grateful for my blessed life!

Written by Bernadette Spitale

36

Little Bird of Fear

One of the ways God can communicate with us is through dreams. Sometimes upon awakening we may not remember the specifics but know we had one. If you still make the effort to write down the dream in times like these the memories will often return.

One morning I woke from a dream. Upon waking I could not recall specifics of the dream so I decided to just begin writing. I started with: I dreamed...... I found as I started to write, the dream slowly started to come back to me and the more I wrote, the more I remembered. It was a long dream and in it I was searching for my friend that I had gotten separated from. I paused for a moment and was contemplating the meaning of this dream when a thought or voice came to me, which said "When there is a brain injury, you can't fly." At the time I understood this to mean when there is fear you can not spiritually, as Soul, go into the higher worlds or truly be yourself.

Hearing this triggered the recall of another dream I had the same night. In this dream I found a bird lying on its back. He was injured and could not fly. I picked him up and was very careful not to injure him more. I gently cupped him in my hands and sent love and encouragement. I told the little bird he would get better and fly again, which he did. As I wrote this dream in my journal, it reminded me of an actual experience I had just the week before. A small bird flew into my home and got trapped inside. My cat went after him and the bird was full of fear. He flew hitting a window very hard and fell to the ground. Picking him up, I carried him outside but he was paralyzed with fear and could not fly. While holding him in my hands I encouraged him and told him he would be all right. After about ten minutes the little bird flew away.

I knew in that moment that God was communicating very directly to me through my dreams. I am the friend I was separated from in the first dream. Over the years I have lost the "real me" while trying to "fit in" to please others out of fear. I am that little bird that is learning to fly once again. My story came out in a poem.

WINGS OF FLIGHT

There was once a little bird, happy as a lark.
Flew here and flitted there,
    loving life without a care.
Now this little bird, having no fears.
Flew through the open door,
    of a house that was near.
He tried and he tried, this little bird did.
To find the way, but the path was hid.
With each attempt, and every try,
His path was blocked, to the sky.
With each obstacle, his fear increased.
He felt he lost, his life of peace.
He flew hard, and he flew fast.
Right into, a pane of glass.
The little bird fell, to the floor.
Where he could, fly no more.
Breathing hard, and the heart did pound.
He was lifted up, from the ground.
With love and compassion, a voice did say,
"Have faith little bird, you're okay."
"Have no fear, and you will fly."
With those words, of love he cried.
Then with peace in his heart,
    and light and sound.
He took flight, and left the ground!

Written by Nancy Cumpston

37

A Year of Healing Dreams

❦

Sometimes the circumstances of a relationship that ends do not afford us the opportunity to speak in person afterwards and come to a place of closure and healing. Fortunately, God can bring us together spiritually in dreams to resolve any remaining issues, heal our wounds, and move forward with peace.

After the end of a difficult relationship with someone I loved but was not able to live with anymore, I had a series of healing dreams. These dreams made it possible for both of us to forgive one another and move on to healthier and happier lives.

We had been together for eight years and had acquired property together. Deciding to end our relationship was the last resort. We tried counseling, life coaching workshops, and other means to heal our relationship. None of that worked. The love was still there but there was no more trust. A betrayal had made it impossible to continue our partnership. Although I knew that I needed to move out and move on, I could not seem to shake the guilt and sadness of this break up. We were not able to communicate with each other after the trust was gone and still to this day have not had contact in the physical. I began to pray to God for help so I could move on and heal. That night I had an experience on the inner planes during a dream. It was very vivid and real.

This Soul and I were in a vast open desert world and we were in light bodies. We still had our human forms but the bodies were made of sparkling light. We were facing one another and a great wave of love cascaded between us. No words were spoken. I woke up from this experience and I felt much more at peace about our decision. I had less guilt and had insights into how we accomplished what we were meant to in our relationship in this lifetime. For the first time, I did not feel like we had wasted all those years. Everything seemed in perfect order and right on schedule.

During the course of that year I had several similar dreams. I eventually had a dream that showed me the original cause of our need to go through this difficult experience together. It happened in another lifetime. From time to time

I still have dreams and we are able to speak kindly to one another. The strong emotions and attachments are gone. We genuinely wish one another well.

Many years after this series of healing dreams I got validation of what my heart knew to be true during retreats at Guidance for a Better Life. I realized that we had indeed both had a healing. They did not happen in my mind, they were very real. I know that as messy as all of it looked, it was perfect. Old karma was resolved between us and I had gained wisdom and a greater capacity to love, which I brought into my new relationship. The series of inner experiences (dreams) and the understanding of them led to closure in what might have been an endless pattern of pain between two Souls. I am very grateful.

Written by Tash Canine

38

Shackled to Ball and Chain

Your ability to grow spiritually is directly proportional to your ability to accept truth. This can be more difficult when it is about yourself and not flattering. However, if you wish to be freed of the things holding you back you have to first be able to accept they are there.
The truth will set you free.

About a year and a half ago, I had a life changing healing by God's Grace. For several months I had been in a funk. I knew something was off but I did not know what it was or how to fix it. I wanted to make changes in my life – switching jobs, moving, etc. I was caught up in thinking only about myself and my actions were reflecting my self-indulgence. Spiritually, I was lazy and acting like a juvenile. I was spinning my wheels spiritually and felt like I was stuck. When you stop moving forward spiritually, you can not stay in one place, you tend to slide backwards; that is exactly what I was doing. I was allowing negative thoughts into my consciousness and these were turning into a self-fulfilling prophecy.

During a retreat at Guidance for a Better Life my teacher lovingly pointed out to me how I had allowed my foggy thinking to get me "into a real pickle." He gave me a lot of truth about myself and with God's help, I was able to hear the truth and begin to accept it. The clear truth from my teacher was an answer to a prayer that had been in my heart. Even though I was not fully aware of how much of a mess I had created with my negative thoughts, I knew I needed help from the Divine and God read my heart.

After class was over for the evening, I walked down to the pond and sat on a bench. I sang HU for a while and begged for the Divine to help me learn this lesson, see more clearly, and begin moving forward spiritually again. I wanted to overcome this "hiccup" and put it in the past. When I stopped talking, I then saw a shackle around my neck, with a long chain and a ball attached to it. I saw the bright white Light of God around me, and then it became more intense and focused. It looked like a laser beam. The laser beam of God's Love burned through the shackle that was around me and I was released. I surrendered whatever the ball and shackle represented to the Divine and knew that I had been given a gift from God. If I were to focus on that shackle and feel bad for whatever it was it would have been counterproductive and self-indulgent.

I still do not know to this day what the shackle was and I am fine with that. By the Divine grace of God, I was free. God read my heart and also heard my prayer that night. I am no longer caught up by my foggy thinking and am spiritually growing and moving forward again.

Thank you God for hearing all of my prayers and answering those in my best interest.

Written by Michelle K. Reuschling

39

Answering the Call

Whether physically young or old you are first and
foremost Soul, an eternal spiritual being here to learn
more about love. None of the ups and downs of life will
ever change this. This is also true of your neighbor, so
find time to love one another. Listening
with an open heart qualifies.

Early one Sunday morning I drove to the store
for an errand. Part way there I got a sudden
nudge to turn the car immediately into another
store. I only had about a two second window to
decide whether to turn or not. Had I passed the
turn I would probably have kept on going to my
original destination, without giving it a second
thought.

Throughout my years at Guidance for a Better
Life, I have learned to listen and trust these
quiet, often subtle, tuggings at my heart. In the
past I often let my agenda and my itinerary
override input from the Divine. But time after

time I had experienced and heard others who benefited from following an inner nudge. Spirit speaks to us continually to guide, protect, and to offer us opportunities to help others. I said, "Yes" without hesitating, accepting the adventure.

I went into the store, not knowing what to expect, but knowing there must be some reason to be here. An elderly man was handing out flyers by the door. We did not make eye contact, but I wondered if he was the reason for my nudge to enter the store. Not sure where to go from here, I stopped at the customer service area near the entrance and began to look over one of the weekly specials, listening for further guidance from the Prophet. I felt drawn to this man, feeling like there was an opportunity to interact with him, so I began walking towards him. I was not sure what I would say or how he would react. He must have felt it too, because he bridged the short distance between us and handed me a flyer. I greeted him and we began to chat.

It seemed like he had been waiting a long time to talk with someone. I wondered how many times I encountered other Souls without ever really acknowledged them, accepting what they offered with no further thought. Bypassing any of the usual introductions or social niceties, the man began to speak to me, Soul to Soul. I listened. His wife had died ten years ago, he told me, and he couldn't afford to live off of social security. An inner nudge encouraged me to remain open to what he had to share. I had never met this man before but he shared with me as easily as if we had known one another for years. He had turned eighty-four last June and he'd been in this area since he was fourteen years old. He happily recalled working on a farm for six dollars a week and buying a new suit for only seven dollars. The time he recalled was such a different world. A strong survival instinct is one of Soul's many qualities. This man had done what he needed to adapt. Still, there were challenges and struggles.

As he continued to share with me, he put his hand on my shoulder, pulling me closer to him as if he did not want to let go of the moment. He had tears in his eyes that he kept wiping away with a tissue in his other hand. I was not viewing him as the shell he had worn these many decades. Instead I heard and saw the glowing spark of God, which he truly is. He welcomed me to come visit him again. I left, feeling peaceful.

The joy of following Spirit, of completing the adventure, left me feeling grateful for my encounter. I doubt the man remembered me after that, but I still think of him years later. It was a gift for me to meet this Soul who had heartbreaks and joys that punctuated the story of his life. Balancing survival in the physical world while growing in awareness of the boundless world of Spirit is the story of Soul. His story was beautiful and I was blessed to hear it.

I gained two insights, two pearls of wisdom from this experience. First, there is so much more to our, and others, experiences. How often do we stop at the surface when looking at life? When we take the time to leave our bubble of safety and comfort we can really see people for who they are, Soul. This is very doable in the everyday hustle and bustle of our busy lives when we remember to tune in and let that still small voice within guide us. Second, when we listen as Soul, we listen with more than our limited physical senses. Responding to these quiet calls of Spirit, we open the doorway for others to share their hearts.

Written by Chris Comfort

40

My Daughter Born
by Spirit

*Many times we are overly attached to a particular
outcome or way of doing something without even
knowing it. The more attached we are the more we tie
God's Hands in delivering His blessings. When we truly
let go the situation can be born anew.*

I am blessed to be the mom of three amazing,
and beautiful girls. Eleven years ago, this journey
of motherhood began. I loved being pregnant
with my first child. Excitement, anticipation,
worry, and joy all coexisting while we awaited
her arrival. Being holistically minded, it was my
deep desire to have a natural childbirth. My
loving husband and I prepared as much as we
possibly could, reading a plethora of books, and
taking every birthing class offered in our area.

The big day was finally approaching. On June
7th, at 2:15 PM my water broke, and with it some

complications arose. I was admitted to the hospital before labor truly began. A natural birth was still on the table, but as time ticked on, the outlook was looking less likely. I relied on the HU, one of my best spiritual tools to keep me calm. I felt peace and knew all would be fine. Five hundred miles away my sister-in-law was also waiting with anticipation. She kept checking in to see how labor was progressing. We went through the entire next day, and still no baby.

Exhausted at this point I gave in and they administered drugs to speed up labor. I finally yielded and accepted an epidural for the intense pain that the labor brings on. On the evening of June 8th true labor was finally setting in. My sister-in-law went to bed that evening with us in her thoughts. She had a dream, and in that dream she saw a brilliant blue light gently push the baby from my womb. Meanwhile back at the hospital, at the exact same moment, I looked at my husband and said, "I need help, I need help, and I truly surrender!"

I felt a sudden and noticeable warmth in my womb and instantly had a rush of stamina. On June 9th at 2:15 AM, exactly thirty-six hours to the minute of my water breaking, we gazed eyes upon our sweet baby girl. It was the Light of God that touched my baby and helped her come into this world. Even though earlier in the day I sang HU, and I felt peace, I still had an attachment to the way I wanted things to work out. I was not even aware of my attachments until I verbally surrendered the outcome. My sister-in-law's dream confirmed what I was feeling in those same moments. In my hour of need God heard my cry and gave me one of the greatest joys of my life; my daughter.

Written by Kate Hall

41

God Touched My Heart

You are loved by God and one of His desires is for you to know and live in this love daily. With the Prophet as your guide you can spiritually travel into the Heavens and experience this love from an aspect of the Divine for yourself — before the end of this physical life. Many who have been blessed to experience God's Love directly have one thing in common — they desire for you to experience it as well.

It was while I was deep in contemplation that I was blessed with an amazing experience of Divine Love. It was given to me after singing HU, an ancient name for God, for a good length of time. As I sat with my physical eyes closed, my attention on the inner reality within me, I was aware of my spiritual teacher who I know as the Prophet, right beside me. He guided the real eternal me, Soul, higher and higher through world upon world of God's creation, the house of many mansions that Jesus spoke of two thousand years ago. The Prophet took me all the way home to the Abode of God Himself. I can best describe it as an expanse of God's Love and Mercy, one so vast that it was like a boundless ocean.

To be allowed to consciously return to my true home where God created me as Soul was a profound gift in and of itself. Yet God always has more love to give, for amid the ocean waves of God's Love, there appeared the Lord Himself in a form that I could relate to, one more personal than the boundless Ocean. The Lord placed His Hand on my heart and held it there. His eternal Love poured into me and I knew beyond any shadow of a doubt that God truly loves me and has always loved me. Without conditions and without judgments He loves me. It is a love that has no beginning and no end. During that moment I knew that His Love is eternal and that it is personal, for God knows me and loves me just as much as any other part of His creation, and He loves me just as I am. I did not earn this gift but I was blessed to be able to receive it by the Grace of the Lord.

In the years since this Divine blessing of blessings there have been many times when I have not felt as loved as I did during that moment in eternity. Love is more than a feeling, for when I remember this blessing of standing before God as He touched me, I know that whether or not I feel loved, God loves me, and that all is well as I walk in His Love. This gift of God touching my heart, for which I thank the Prophet, the one whom God has ordained to take Soul home to Him, is a blessing that was not given to me just for my own benefit, or to be hoarded selfishly like a prized possession. This gift of Divine love has blessed me with a greater capacity to give and receive love. It has helped to liberate me from selfish desires and to think more of the needs of others and to be able to truly hear and know in my heart what God, through His Prophet, is asking me to do. I also know that the love was given to me so that I can testify to this: God is real and God loves you.

Written by Roland Vonder Muhll

42

Love the Lord With All Your Heart

❦

The simple but profound truth is, you exist because God loves you. It is one thing to have someone tell you this — it is quite another to have a spiritual guide who can help you come to know this truth for yourself. Joy and abundance beyond measure are available when you personally experience God's Love.

"And he answering said, Thou shalt love the Lord thy God with all thy heart, and with all thy soul, and with all thy strength, and with all thy mind; and thy neighbor as thyself." Luke 10:27 KJV

My fervent prayer as a child and young adult was to truly know that God loves me and how to love God, not just in my mind. I wanted to come before God through love, not through fear and guilt that many churches promote. One of my very favorite passages in the Bible was about loving God with all your heart, mind, and Soul.

This passage has been tucked away in my heart. It always was clear to me that one of Jesus' key messages was that God, His Father, is love and how much we are loved and the importance of loving others as ourselves. In everyday life I had a hard time loving myself and was harder on myself than others. Not being able to love myself it was difficult to accept God's Love, though it was always there for me. This sense of unworthiness dogged me much of my life.

In 1998 I was guided to at Guidance for a Better Life. Over the years my spiritual teacher, who is a true Prophet of God, gradually guided me through every angle possible, a 360-degree view, to experience how much I am loved, and that I am worthy of God's Love. God loves us all, every one of us unconditionally. I learned that we are here on Earth to learn about giving and receiving love. I learned and began to experience the amazing inner joy of reaching out to others, instead of only thinking about myself.

A priceless experience was gifted to me a few years ago; one I treasure and hope to remember in my heart forever. It took place shortly after one of my friends, also a student of Del's, had shared a facilitation at a retreat that was full of love. There was a sense of expectant joy in the air as Del returned to the front of the room. The Prophet suggested, "Let's come together, be really together for a moment. Let go; surrender with the inner Prophet's assistance." I/we merged into a gigantic white light ball which got brighter and brighter. I was aware of the particles of light, sparks of individuality within the greater light ball (God's Light). "In this moment you have everything you need." And I felt my cares, everything melt away. And the more I surrendered, let go, the boundaries of various boxes that had contained my limited concept of God faded away and my awareness of the limitlessness and expansiveness of the gigantic white light ball grew and grew.

"Just be." I experienced a stillness, deep peace, and Divine Love. I felt totally nourished in that moment of eternity and had everything I needed. As the love became more intense, I accepted it, almost overpowering, and felt so much love for God. The flow back and forth between God's Heart and my heart intensified until it became a crescendo of golden waves of love crashing upon the shores of my heart. My heart was bursting with love for God. In that moment of eternity, I only wanted to love and praise God forever. In that moment as Soul I experienced my favorite Bible passage... "to love the Lord God with all my heart, mind, and Soul."

Written by Jan Reid

43

Divine Healing After Divorce

❧

Within the Heavenly realms exist spiritual temples. Places where the truth of God is kept pure, safe from the polluting minds of men. With the proper guide you can spiritually travel to these sacred temples to gain in wisdom, understanding, or in the following case, to receive healing. The price of admission — an open heart.

Divorce can be a difficult experience that may take one a while to work through on different levels. For me it took time and was a process of grieving, healing, and learning to let go. Divine Spirit helped me work through this difficult period. I was given many dreams and other inner experiences in a positive and constructive way. They helped me to keep my heart open, be fair, and honest when interacting with my former husband and sincerely wish him well in his life ahead.

A major healing came while I was at a 3-Day Spiritual Retreat at Guidance for a Better Life. Del, my spiritual teacher who is a true Prophet of God, was guiding us on an inner experience where we were blessed with a sacred opportunity. We were spiritually taken to visit one of the spiritual temples that exist in the vast inner worlds of God. These temples are a place where Souls can go to learn, be healed, gain insight, or have other experiences that help them in some way, but one can only get there if taken by an authorized agent of God.

As Del guided us to the temple in our Soul bodies, I noticed a sense of lightness like I was flying. I trusted him, so although this was like exploring new spiritual territory, I did not hesitate to follow. I arrived in what looked like a large rotunda with many arched windows and velvet tapestry. Light streamed into the room from all directions. It was not ordinary physical light, it was the Light of God that illuminated the temple. There was a podium that looked like it should hold a holy book, but instead there was a fountain on it. My former husband was there, he cupped his hands, took water from the fountain and poured it over his head. I looked down at his ankle and heard four links of a chain that had

145

been there fall to the floor. I went to the fountain and did the same, taking some of its living water and poured it over my head. He helped me dry my face and we agreed that all was as it should be as we journeyed separately on our own paths. I said goodbye to him as we left.

This occurred nearly four years after our divorce. God knows us better than we know ourselves. Although outwardly I had gone on with my life, I was still attached at some level and afraid to let go. This experience was a healing one because afterwards, I felt as if I was able to release something I was holding onto. The chain links falling to the floor made me think that perhaps past life karmic ties between us may have also been undone as well. I do not think I could fully comprehend all that happened, but I know the magnitude of the blessings were awesome. I felt freedom, strength, and had courage to move on. The healing waters of the fountain, an aspect of Divine Spirit, originate in the Abode of God, the source of God's unlimited Love and Mercy. It was truly out of God's great Love and bountiful Grace and mercy that this miraculous healing could take place when I was ready, and it was through the Prophet that this became so.

I treasure this sacred experience and the very real impact it had on my life. This was an important turning point for me. I am ever grateful for the Prophet's inner and outer spiritual guidance that helped resolve the situation in a way that was mutually beneficial to my former husband and me. I am so appreciative of the ways he helped me keep an open heart, soothe the pain, guide me through the grieving process, and let go of unnecessary entanglements. Being able to finally move forward with confidence and being at peace with the past was indeed a very precious gift. Thank you!

Written by Lorraine Fortier

44

Golden Robe Saves a Life

It is in Soul's nature to care about the well-being of those we love. How can we pray for someone without trying to control their life or presume we know what is in their best spiritual interest? The following is a great example of helping without trying to control or presume to know what is best for another.

Some years ago a beloved relative, a young woman, was dating a young man. Over time it appeared their relationship was unhealthy, and while I did not know for certain, I suspected he was abusive in some way. I sensed that something was different about her after she got involved in this relationship. She was making some very unusual choices that were altering her life and was lying about them. She abruptly dropped out of college, detached herself from a loving family, and moved to a distant town with her boyfriend. Loved ones, especially her parents, were distraught over the situation.

I too was concerned for her safety and well-being but did not want to interfere with her life. After all she was an adult and was supposed to be capable of making her own choices. I generally do not get involved in the personal affairs of others because I do not want to encroach uninvited, but I love her dearly and wanted to help her in some way. I did not know what to do, so I asked God for help. I wished her the best and hoped she was truly happy with her decisions and lifestyle, but if she was unhappy and trapped in a bad situation, I prayed for God to protect her and let her know that she is loved.

One day I sang HU, a love song to God, and reflected on a recent experience during a guided contemplation at Guidance for a Better Life. During the spiritual exercise I received a beautiful golden robe from the Heavens above. Del, my teacher, helped me understand this gifted robe is a source of God's loving comfort and protection to the one who wears it. During this time of reflection, I also thought of this young woman, and a trusted spiritual teacher took me spiritually to visit her. I saw her sitting on a couch watching television but she did not recognize our presence. I sat on the couch with her for some time and simply expressed love to her. Divine love filled the entire room. I had a nudge and desire in my heart to give her the golden robe for comfort and protection should she ever need it. Guided by the spiritual teacher, I gently placed the golden robe around her shoulders and gave her a hug. I wished that she could accept this special gift and turned over the outcome to the Divine. After all, God knows exactly what we need and when we need it.

Over the next several days and weeks she occasionally appeared in my dreams or contemplations where I gently expressed to her how much she is loved. Sometimes I saw her enveloped in a glowing blue bubble of light, which is another form of Divine protection. Several months later I received a phone call with news that the young woman feared for her safety in this abusive relationship and wanted to come home. This was a special day because Divine Spirit arranged a narrow window of opportunity setting the circumstances for her safe return home to her family. The timing that day was perfect in several ways. Her mother is typically not home during the day, but she was home that day to receive the call. It happened to be the first time in months that she talked to her parents. A snowstorm was forecast for that day but was late arriving, which allowed for safe travel conditions. When her parents arrived to pick her up, the boyfriend was conveniently away from the house, which averted a possible confrontation.

God's Love and protection saved this young woman's life, and I am blessed to witness it and be a part of it. God loves each of his children and has a desire for us to share this love with each other. Divine love and grace conditioned her with the courage, strength, and opportunity to come home that day. The timing of events, the brief window of opportunity, and all the seemingly random "coincidences" were truly miracles, the Hand of God, working in her life. Over time Divine love continued to heal the emotional scars of her experience and nurture a lasting love connection with her family. This is a testimony to the power of God's Love.

Written by Chris Hibshman

45

Family Reunion in Heaven

A family prays to send love and comfort to a loved one who has just passed away. They all three were blessed to witness her arrival in Heaven. The following testimony is one perspective of the joyous reunion.

Aunt Mildred was one of those delightful ladies who was always cheerful and a pleasure to talk with. I admired her strength and her attitude to be happy and enjoy life. Her husband and sister, who was my grandmother, passed away several years ago. Because her health was failing she stayed in an assisted living facility. She recently had gotten the flu and was very ill.

It was a Sunday afternoon when my sister-in-law called to tell us that Aunt Mildred had passed. My husband and our two children sat together and sang HU, asking the Prophet to bless her during this time of transition. As I sang HU and was in contemplation I saw a beautiful field of green grass with rolling hills beyond. In the distance I saw a beautiful white city, with tall white spires. In the field, family and friends who were already in Heaven gathered with joy and excitement to welcome Aunt Mildred.

As she walked towards the group, her smile was huge, and her eyes were bright with joy and wonder. As she came close to her deceased husband Chet, he stood still for a moment. He looked as though he had a lump in his throat; so overcome with emotion that he could not move or speak. Then he took a step towards her and she paused for a moment, tilted her head a bit as she looked at him sweetly, and then they embraced tightly, as though they would never let each other go. Grandma stood beside them in anticipation to welcome her sister. They embraced and then Aunt Mildred smiled broadly as she looked up to see the next person to welcome her. Grandma turned to me with eyes very bright and loving, and as I hugged her I must have said, "I love you Grandma," for she said to me, "I love you too dear" in her sweet loving voice. Those were the last words that we had said to each other just before she had died several years earlier. It was as though we picked up right where we had left off!

One by one all of my family members in Heaven came over to see me and I got to hug each one. Grandpa shook my hand vigorously, just like he did when I was a little girl. He was laughing and his eyes sparkled with merriment. My dad, who had died twenty-five years earlier, looked young and healthy as he smiled at me, taking in how I had grown up since we were last together. As I hugged my other grandpa he slipped a black olive into my hand. I was delighted to experience that again, since I had forgotten that he would do that for my brother and me at family dinners. I noticed that he looked much younger and appeared very healthy and vigorous. I realized that when we were all together on Earth, my family seldom hugged each other. Here in Heaven everyone was joyously embracing. Perhaps here they were freed from hang-ups and had learned something about expressing love. In Heaven there is much more to experience than playing harps in fluffy white clouds!

I prayed for the Prophet to bless the gathering and he appeared. Everyone turned to look at him and they gasped in awe. Being in his presence was a huge blessing and they knew that this was very special. After the Prophet left no one spoke a word for a while, for they were so awed by being in his presence.

Later I introduced my husband and children to their relatives whom they had not met in this lifetime. It was such a joyous, happy occasion, and it was beautiful to see Aunt Mildred with her loved ones again, and to see her healthy and happy. And then there was even another blessing, as our cat Tigger, who had died a few years earlier walked by. The whole experience was blessings upon blessings! Thank you Prophet for making this possible. It was a joy and a comfort for me to see them all happy and well, and to know that Aunt Mildred was OK and was welcomed into a new life.

Written by Diane Kempf

46

I Am Free to Be Me

One of the greatest attributes Soul has been created with is the ability to communicate with God. Having this constant lifeline of love and guidance as you go through your day can make life a joy to live. All Souls have the potential for this communication but it must be nurtured. Similar to when learning a new language, it takes time and is much easier when you have a teacher who is fluent.

Lately I have been looking back in my life and realizing the hand of the Divine and Its loving presence has been with me all along. The presence of an inner guide or inner teacher has been right there with me guiding and protecting me all through my life. As I grew in strength spiritually, I began to recognize and notice the Divine presence of the Holy Spirit in every incident and aspect of my life! God has a plan custom designed just for ME!

I first learned about the constant presence of the Prophet during retreats at Guidance for a

Better Life. I learned the Voice of God, Holy Spirit, was working through him! It was astounding to know God knows my every thought and prayer! At first I was very weak at this recognition. It was like making a commitment to exercise, to get in physical shape! I worked with the skills I learned at the retreat center, very weak at first. As the weakness faded the inner part of the Prophet's presence grew stronger. As His presence grew stronger I began to have one-sided conversations with the Divine, my side at first! Over time I talked to God and began to LISTEN. Now as I listened to the inner guidance I could hear suggestions coming through, solutions, and long sought answers. Sometimes when I first awaken I will receive an insight to a question I asked the night before.

I learned and became skilled at how my night and awake dreams were customized to help me understand an answer to a prayer. They were alerting me to a solution I was seeking. Sometimes a seemingly random conversation was of importance, even a license plate word would be of significance, a clue to what I had asked. I grew to understand even the timing of an answer was of great value. I was now ready to hear what was in my best interest, always knowing I still had free will to choose.

The confidence I have now, the knowingness, the really knowing with all my heart God hears me is a gateway to a life filled with love and freedom to be just me! It is a comfort beyond all measure. I will ask you this; what if God knows you so well that he knows your every thought and prayer? What if He hears and knows your every word and deed? How would you live your life? Would you live it differently? Would you be grateful to know how very much you are loved and guided?

I know God loves me just the way I am or I would not exist. And to recognize He hears and knows me so personally, better than I know myself, and really cares how my life progresses is a very extraordinary gift. The blessings in my life are endless since I woke up and recognized the loving presence of the Prophet in my life and the personal closeness we have developed together.

I love my life!

Written by Nancy Nelson

47

A Place for Us in God's Mansion

The following is a beautiful dream experience that serves as a reminder — there is a place for all of us. What a comfort it is to know this.

One night after singing HU, a love song to God, and asking God to help me accept more Divine love, I was blessed with a very special dream. In the dream I was allowed to live in a beautiful mansion. It was not my mansion but I was allowed to live there. It was God's mansion and there was a place for me. I excitedly explored the rooms that were open. There was a kitchen, a bathroom, a bedroom for my children, and several hallways and entryways. The house was furnished with furniture, painted art, ancient vases, and more. The craftsmanship of the construction was gorgeous and far surpassed any physical home I have ever seen. It was not gaudy or flashy. It was handcrafted and built with every detail as important as the next.

During the dream the door to a new room that I had seen but never gone in was opened for me. It was a dressing room that had a large mirror at the top of several steps and the walls had a built-in armoire for jewelry. Every piece of jewelry had its own drawer and even the drawer handles and wood had an exquisite level of detail. Each room had so much detail and beauty that they could not be fully explored in a lifetime. I was so excited in the dream to keep exploring and was trying to absorb everything I saw. I then realized that I was only seeing a portion of the house and that there were gardens and areas to explore outside the house as well. Knowing that there was so much more beyond what I was seeing was such an awesome realization. I was so eager to continue discovering new rooms and areas.

When I awoke from this dream I felt alive and alert and also comforted and reassured but most of all loved. The dream spoke to me of the biblical quote about the many mansions in my Father's house. God wants to draw nigh with His children and the dream was showing me that I have a safe and special place to call home. There is a place for all of God's children in the home of God. There is so much to learn and experience in God's Heavens and we are so blessed to be welcomed.

The dream also reminded me that there is always more to learn and more growth on my spiritual journey. The rooms symbolized consciousness and how over time our view of the world expands and we can operate from a higher vantage point. In the dream my brother and sister-in-law and I were starting to give tours of the mansion to share the experience with others. It was a joy to serve others by showing them around the beautiful mansion.

This dream has stayed with me... the excitement to explore and keep learning, the beauty and love in every detail of the mansion, the comfort and security I felt being there, and knowing on a deeper level that my true home is in the Heart of God. I look forward to possibly having another dream where I am able to explore more rooms and continue to open the door for more tours.

Written by Catherine Hughes

48

God Intervened

There is no limit to the ways God can bestow His Love and protection on those in need. The following is an amazing example of this.

Years ago, as a young adult Boy Scout leader, I was driving a vanload of boys at the start of a camping trip. Sometime after dark, we pulled up to the stop sign on a country road. In the distance I could see the single headlight of an oncoming motorcycle. I believed the motorcycle was still quite far away and moving rather slowly, but my observation turned out to be wrong. As I turned onto the main road, I suddenly realized the motorcycle was much closer than I had believed.

As I floored the van's gas pedal, the boys in the back of the van yelled in fright as the bike moved in very close. Then in wonder and amazement, they described that they saw a great hand, made of light, reach out and keep the bike from hitting the back of the van. The Hand of God intervened to keep several lives safe that night.

Since that time, I have come to find and welcome the Divine presence in all areas of my life. As I have become more aware of God, I have experienced more love, help, healing, peace, rest, suggestions for creating a more abundant life, and so much more. I hope you will come to welcome God into your life and to see the wonderful changes that are possible.

Written by Timothy C. Donley

49

Journey to Tibet

If this beautifully written piece does not excite and inspire you with grand possibilities, then I do not know what will. There is so, so much more to everyday waking life. If you seek to understand life's mysteries and embrace the truths of God, the Prophet is the one that can show you the way.

Fresh snow danced across the huge stone steps leading up to the doorway of an ancient Tibetan monastery. The jagged peaks of the Himalayan Mountains towered around us silhouetted by the fading evening light. Slowly, the temple door opened.

My body was thousands of miles away sitting peacefully in Virginia. Our spiritual journey was being guided by Del Hall. After singing HU, a love song to God, my consciousness had shifted naturally away from my body much like in a dream, to the distant Tibetan evening. Del's whole group waited excitedly on the stone steps. This is a very real place; our spiritual journey had brought us here in full consciousness.

An ancient monk clothed in white reverently greeted Del by the immense wooden doorway. They spoke for a moment and observed our group of newcomers. As the door opened it revealed a massive rotunda bursting with light. The light filled my being with hope, reverence, and love. This was no ordinary light. It was the Light of God. As the light shone upon our group I felt it purify, uplift, and nourish me spiritually. Clearly this was no ordinary temple. It was a true Temple of God, ordained and sustained by Him directly, unspoiled by the hand of man, and accessible to man only under the guidance of a true Prophet of God.

Del and the white-robed monk led us into the temple. Our small group paused just inside the door, absorbing the scene with awe. Workers in the temple moved purposefully about the rotunda busy in the responsibilities of this sacred sanctuary. The light seemed to come from everywhere at once, filling every corner and leaving no shadows. I watched the white-robed monk ascend a beautifully curved staircase, his hand upon an ornate golden banister.

He observed our group steadily. Slowly his gaze met mine and he spoke a single word: "Love." The energy in his voice entered my heart like an arrow! The single word spoke more than many volumes of literature, more than any eloquent speech. It was more than a syllable, more than a word. A mountain of wisdom and meaning surged behind it. It reached deep within me, speaking to the innermost part of my being, Soul, the true self.

The power of his message still reverberating within me, a gentle hand touched my arm. A worker from the temple led me to a hidden staircase descending into the foundation of the temple. He motioned me forward and I walked carefully down the stairs. Before me hung a narrow rope bridge leading to a stone platform. In the middle of the platform a small fire burned. And on the other side of the fire was the white-robed monk himself, sitting hooded and cross-legged. Behind him stood two full bookshelves holding ancient texts from forgotten kingdoms.

I crossed the bridge eagerly, but with a slow and measured pace. I sat across the fire from him and his deep gray eyes met mine. Immeasurable love and peace emanated from him. Not a word was spoken but I found myself drawn into his eyes, like an invisible force pulling me into another world. I traveled into his eyes as Soul. Everything changed; eternity seemed to exist in a moment. The Temple Guardian's endless eyes became my entire universe. Love was everywhere, but not love as I had known it before, it was a love that transcended emotion, time, religion, everything. I had truly experienced God's Love. In the days following this experience I was able to share it with the group. Others had similar experiences, personalized for their own spiritual growth. Del guided me in understanding these sacred events. He told me that this teacher had used a single word, such as "Love," to teach others before. Since the retreat the word he spoke has unfolded into hundreds of different nuances and applications.

Del explained that the basement seemed to represent the "cave of fire," a spiritual rite of passage that all seekers must go through on their journey home to God. This is a period of great trial and tribulation. This proved to be an accurate interpretation, for the next several years were a period of intense honesty and self-discovery. This was not always easy! But it led to a state of greater peace, freedom, and stability. Somewhat, one might say, like crossing the narrow rope bridge in the temple onto the solid stone platform.

This took place during my first spiritual retreat at Guidance for a Better Life. In the ten years that have followed, it became clear that this was only the tip of the iceberg.

Written by David Hughes

50

In Our Father's Eyes

This is an amazing testimony on visiting the Abode of God. Traveling spiritually in full consciousness to the source of all — to the home of Our Father. Guided there by the Prophet to receive healing, revelation, comfort, and a profound insight — we are each loved unconditionally by God. Being able to accept this love changes everything.

Do you know that we are welcome in Heaven? Do you know that God loves you no matter what you are facing in life? Out of the many, many blessings that being a student of Del's has given me, this following experience stands out as the one that gave me an understanding that God's Love for us truly has no conditions. Knowing this has given me a peace that has changed how I walk through life.

Some years ago, I was going through a time where I was struggling with jealousy and envy. I was not comfortable in my own skin, and thought that if I was more like someone else or had what they had in their lives, then I would be happy. While logically, I knew that this was unhealthy, I could not seem to shake it. In my eyes, I was not deserving of love.

During a week-long spiritual retreat at Guidance for a Better Life Del led us in singing HU. After some time, I became aware that I was in front of a huge ocean made entirely of God's Love. Instinctively, I knelt. I was not alone. Beside me were Souls as far as I could see. Each one of us was made of glowing, shimmering light. Each one of us was beautiful. We were each kneeling along this beach in love and reverence to Our Heavenly Father. As I looked out over the wide expanse, I saw pure white light reflecting in the distant water. The light came closer to me and I saw a form appear sitting in a gigantic chair. The Heavenly Father was seated before us. I could see and feel our love going out to Him with each HU, and then returning back to us in a beautiful rhythm.

As I was kneeling before this immense ocean of God's Love, I was experiencing such a deep, deep peace. I have never experienced this much peace in my life. I needed nothing and I lacked nothing. Peace filled every fiber of my being.

Tears streamed down my face, as I accepted the love that was being offered to me. Then, Our Heavenly Father arose and came towards me across the water. With such a gentleness, He lifted my head and kissed my forehead. "I love you and I am glad you are here." His eyes filled the sky, immense and loving. His Love continued to pour into me, filling every part of me.

I knew then, as I do now, that He loves me without conditions. He has the same love for you, no matter what you are struggling with inside or going through in life. Our Father truly loves us unconditionally, and accepting this love truly changes us.

For days, and now years later, I close my eyes and return to this living experience of God's Love. Seeing the love in my Heavenly Father's eyes, face to face, gave me a confidence in His Love for me that is unshakable. Thank you Del, the Prophet, for guiding me home to Heaven to meet Our Father, face to face.

Written by Molly Comfort

Guidance for a Better Life
Our Story

❧

My Father's Journey

God always has a living Prophet on Earth to teach His Ways and accomplish His will. My father, Del Hall III, is currently God's true Prophet fully raised up and ordained by God Himself. He was not always a Prophet, nor did he even know what a Prophet was, but God had a

Prophet Del Hall III

plan for him like He has for all of His children. Over many years through many life experiences, God had begun to prepare my father for his future assignment, mostly unbeknownst to him. Everything he experienced in his life from the joys to the sadness helped prepare him for his future role as Prophet.

My dad grew up in California and was a decent student but a better athlete. He received an appointment to the United States Naval Academy in Annapolis, Maryland where he later met my mother. They were married two days after he graduated and received his commission as an officer. After a short tour on a Navy ship deployed to Vietnam, he went to flight training school and became a Navy fighter pilot. While attending flight school in Pensacola, Florida he also earned a Master of Science Degree and had the first of his three children, a son. After flight school he was stationed in a fighter squadron on the East Coast, where he and my mom began investing in real estate, adding to their family with the birth of two daughters. Following this tour of duty he was assigned as a jet flight instructor in Texas, after which, his time in the Navy was finished. He was a natural pilot and loved his time in the sky, but it was time to move on.

So far in life he had no real concern for, or even thought much about God, religion, or spiritual matters in general. He lived life fully. He raised his family. He traveled. He invested and became an entrepreneur starting and growing highly successful businesses in diverse fields ranging from real estate to aerospace consulting. Years before however, a seed had been planted when God's eternal teachings were introduced to him in his late teens, and while it did not show outwardly, the truth in these teachings spoke to his heart. My dad might not have been giving much thought about God up to this point in his life, but God was definitely thinking about him and the future He had planned for him. Like an acorn destined to become a mighty oak, the seed that lay dormant in his heart would someday be stirred to life. Through all his life experiences, both "good" and "bad," God would be preparing him for his future role as His Prophet.

When God decided it was time, He called my dad to Him. He did this by shutting down the world of financial security my dad had built. Over a period of two years all of his businesses were wound down and dissolved. What seemed like security turned out to be an illusion. Financial success had not provided true security. He now had failed businesses and a failing marriage and was trying to fix things without God's help, principles, or guidance. As painful as this time in his life was, it was yet another step towards the glorious life of service awaiting my father. God was removing him from the world my dad had created and furthering him along his path to his future role as Prophet.

After his marriage ended and his businesses wound down, he started fresh by going out west to give flying lessons near Lake Mead, Nevada. While living in Nevada my dad was reintroduced to the eternal teachings of God he first learned of as a teenager twenty-three years earlier, and though they resonated with him at the time, his priorities were different back then. Now, his serious training could begin. He started having very clear experiences with the Holy Spirit and noticed there was a familiarity with these teachings and experiences. He embraced the long hours of instruction, which often lasted until sunrise, and was receptive to the personal spiritual experiences he was given. This began an intense period of study and desire for spiritual truth that continues to this day. Some of his most profound and meaningful experiences during this time were with past Prophets of old. They came to him spiritually in contemplations and dreams. He learned of their roles in history and how they were raised up and ordained by God directly. He began to realize they were training him but was not clear why. A few times his experiences led him to believe he was in training to be a future Prophet. However, that revelation made no sense to him because he felt he was an imperfect person who made mistakes and had failures. He thought of the past and current Prophets of God as perfected Souls, not imperfect like he felt he was. Why would God choose him for such a role? He did not feel qualified.

Besides being introduced to God's teachings while he was out west, my father was blessed to meet his current wife Lynne. Returning to the East Coast, my father and Lynne moved into a small cabin on land he had acquired before his businesses shut down. This was a major change in his life, but it felt deeply right within him. He began to remember a desire to live like this as a child; from early childhood my dad found clarity and peace in nature. He had forgotten about this until now, but God had not and made this dream a reality. In addition to being their home, these beautiful, three-hundred-plus acres of land in the Blue Ridge Mountains would eventually become the location for the Guidance for a Better Life retreat center. The perfection of my father's experiences from earlier in his life in real estate, providing the land for his next step in life, speaks to the perfection of God's plan. One of many many examples I could list.

For many years my dad took wilderness skills courses around the country. He specialized in the study of wild edible and medicinal plants, tracking, and awareness skills, and authored articles for publication. Inspired to help folks feel more comfortable in the outdoors, my dad and Lynne began the Nature Awareness School in 1990. Classes were focused on teaching awareness and the primitive living skills needed to enjoy the woods and survive in them if necessary. An amazing thing happened within those first few years though; students began to experience aspects of God in very personal and dramatic ways. Somewhat like my dad's experience out west, they found that stepping away from their daily routine and the hustle of life, if even for a few days, created space for Spirit to do Its work. Whether they were enjoying the beauty of the Virginia wilderness and tranquility of the school grounds or relaxing by the pond, he found students' hearts opened, and they became more receptive to the Divine Hand that is always reaching out to Its children.

More and more the discourse during wilderness classes shifted to the meanings of dreams, personal growth, finding balance in life, and experiences the students were having with the Voice of God in Its many forms. An increase of spiritual retreats was offered to fulfill the demand and over time became the predominant class offerings; the wilderness survival skills classes eventually fading away completely. The name "Nature Awareness School" seemed to be less fitting for what was actually being taught now and in February 2019 my father changed the name of the retreat center to Guidance for a Better Life.

Throughout this time my father's training and spiritual study continued. My father reached mastership and was ordained by God on July 7, 1999 but he was still not yet Prophet, more was required. On October 22, 2012, twenty-five years since his full-time intensive training had begun, God ordained him as His chosen Prophet, and He has continued to raise him up further since. God works through my father in very direct and beneficial ways for his students. Hundreds and hundreds of students for more than thirty years have received God's eternal teachings through my father's instruction and mentoring. They have had personal experiences with the Divine which have transformed and greatly blessed their lives. My father's greatest joy is being used by God as a servant to share God's ways and truths with thirsty Souls and hungry seekers. In addition to mountaintop retreats, my father continues to spread God's ways and teachings that so greatly blessed his life and the lives of his loved ones in many ways, including his books and videos.

Maybe you are at a turning point in your life and looking for direction. Maybe you have a knowing there is more to life but not sure what that might be or how to find it. Or, maybe you are simply drawn to what you read and hear in our stories. God speaks to our hearts and calls each of us in many different ways. Like my father's journey demonstrates, it doesn't matter where you started or the twists, turns, or seeming dead-ends your life has taken; God wants us to know Him more fully, and for us to know our purpose within His creation. He wants us to experience His Love regardless of our religious path or lack thereof. He always has a living Prophet here on Earth to help us accomplish His desire for us — to show us the way home to Him and to experience more abundance in our lives while we are still living here on Earth. God's Prophet today is my father, Del Hall III. You have the opportunity to grow spiritually through God's teachings which Prophet shares. His guidance for a better life is available for you — please accept it.

Written by Del Hall IV

My Son, Del Hall IV

My son, Del Hall IV, joined Guidance for a Better Life as an instructor after fifteen years of in-class training with me, his father. He helped develop the five-step Keys to Spiritual Freedom Study Program and facilitates the first two courses in the program: Step One

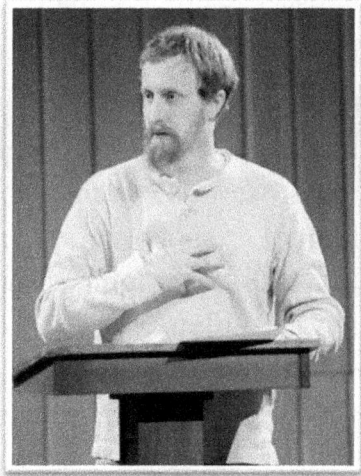

Del Hall IV

"Tools to Recognize Divine Guidance" and Step Two "Understanding Divine Guidance." Del also teaches people about the rich history of dream study and how to better recall their own dreams during the Dream Study Workshops, which he hosts around the country. He is qualified to step in and facilitate any of my retreats should the need arise.

Del authored the book *God is in the Garden*,

a priceless book of wisdom in the form of parables. Through stories of everyday events of life on the mountain Del shares profound insights into the nature of God and life that are infused with his natural humor and unique perspective.

Del is also Vice President of Marketing and helps with everything required to get the "good news" from Guidance for a Better Life out to hungry seekers: everything from book publishing, blogging, and posting on social media outlets. He is co-author and book cover designer for many of our, thus far, twenty published books.

My son loves the opportunity to work on creative projects for Guidance for a Better Life. From a very early age he has been an artist and loved creating artwork in multiple mediums. He was accepted into gifted art programs in Virginia Beach, Virginia and then after high school graduation he attended the School of the Museum of Fine Arts in Boston. He is now a nationally exhibited artist and his *Paintings of the Light and Sound of God* are in over two hundred public and private collections. One of the greatest joys of the painting process for Del is using his paintings as an opportunity to share with others the inspiration behind them, God's Love and his experiences with the Light and Sound of God, the Holy Spirit, in contemplation and in waking life.

Del lives on the retreat center property in the Blue Ridge Mountains of Virginia with his wife where they raised and homeschooled my three grandchildren. Recently he helped me with an extensive renovation and update for the three hand-built log cabins on retreat center property originally used for advanced spiritual retreats. He loves woodworking, tending to his vegetable garden, pruning his fruit trees, and helping maintain the beautiful three-hundred acres of retreat center property for students to enjoy. There is always something that needs attention on the land and Del is always up to the challenge. He loves to travel and spends his free time enjoying this beautiful country with his family in their RV.

My son has had multiple brain surgeries starting when he was seventeen years old for a recurring brain tumor. He credits God for surviving and thriving all this time when most with his condition do not. He looks to the sunrise every day with gratitude for yet another chance at life. With that chance he desires to help me share the love and teachings of God that have so blessed our lives. I pray to God daily thanking Him for my son's good health.

Written by Prophet Del Hall

What is the Role of God's Prophet?

An introductory understanding of God's handpicked and Divinely trained Prophet is necessary to fully benefit from reading this book. God ALWAYS has a living Prophet of His choice on Earth. He has a physical body with a limited number of students, but the inner spiritual side of Prophet is limitless. Spiritually he can help countless numbers of Souls all over the world, no matter what religion or path they are on — even if that is no path at all. He teaches the ways of God and shares the Light and Sound of God. He delivers the living Word of God. Prophet can teach you physically as well as through dreams, and he can lift you into the Heavens of God. He offers protection, peace, teachings, guidance, healing, and love.

Each of God's Prophets throughout history has a unique mission. One may only have a few students with the sole intent to keep God's teachings and truth alive. God may use another to change the course of history. God's Prophets are usually trained by both the current and former Prophets. The Prophet is tested and trained over a very long period of time. The earlier Prophets are physically gone but teach the new Prophet in the inner spiritual worlds. This serves two main purposes: the trainee becomes very adept at spiritual travel and gains wisdom from those in whose shoes he will someday walk. This is vital training because the Prophet is the one who must safely prepare and then take his students into the Heavens and back.

There are many levels of Heaven, also called planes or mansions. Saint Paul once claimed to know a man who went to the third Heaven. Actually it was Paul himself that went, but the pearl is, if there is a third Heaven, it presumes a first and second Heaven also exist. The first Heaven is often referred to as the Astral plane. Even on just that one plane of existence there are over one hundred sub-planes. This Heaven is where most people go after passing, unless they receive training while still here in their physical body. Without a guide who is trained properly in the ways of God a student could misunderstand the intended lesson and become confused as to what is truth. The inner worlds are enormous compared to the physical worlds. They are very real and can be explored safely when guided by God's Prophet.

Part of my mission is to share more of what is spiritually possible for you as a child of God. Few Souls know or understand that God's Prophet can safely guide God's children, while still alive physically, to their Heavenly Home. Taking a child of God into the Heavens is not the job of clergy. Clergy have a responsibility to pass on the teaching of their religion exactly as they were taught, not to add additional concepts or possibilities. If every clergy member taught their own personal belief system no religion could survive for long. Then the beautiful teachings of an earlier Prophet of God would be lost. Clergy can be creative in finding interesting and uplifting ways to share their teachings, but their job is to keep their religion intact. However, God sends His Prophets to build on the teachings of His past Prophets, to share God's Light and Love, to teach His language, and to guide Souls to their Heavenly Home.

There is ALWAYS MORE when it comes to God's teachings and truth. No one Prophet can teach ALL of God's ways. It may be that the audience of a particular time in history cannot absorb more wisdom. It could be due to a

Prophet's limited time to teach and limited time in a physical body on Earth. Ultimately, it is that there is ALWAYS MORE! Each of God's Prophets brings additional teachings and opportunities for ways to draw closer to God, building on the work and teachings of former Prophets. That is one reason why Prophets of the past ask God to send another; to comfort, teach, and continue to help God's children grow into greater abundance. Former Prophets continue to have great love for God's children and want to see them continue to grow in accepting more of God's Love. One never needs to stop loving or accepting help from a past Prophet in order to grow with the help of the current Prophet. All true Prophets of God work together and help one another to do God's work.

All the testimonies in this book were written by students at the Guidance for a Better Life retreat center. It is here that the nature of God, the Holy Spirit, and the nature of Soul are EXPERIENCED under the guidance of a true living Prophet of God. Guidance for a Better Life is NOT a religion, it is a retreat center. God and His Prophet are NOT disparaging of any religion of love. However, the more a path defines itself with its teachings, dogma, or tenets, the more

190

"walls" it inadvertently creates between the seeker and God. Sometimes it even puts God into a smaller box. God does not fit in any box. Prophet is for all Souls and is purposely not officially aligned with any path, but shows respect to all.

YOU can truly have an ABUNDANT LIFE through a personal and loving relationship with God, the Holy Spirit, and God's ordained Prophet. This is my primary message to you. Having a closer relationship with the Divine requires understanding the "Language of the Divine." God expresses His Love to us, His children, in many different and sometimes very subtle ways. Often His Love goes unrecognized and unaccepted because His language is not well known. The testimonies in this book have shown you some of the ways in which God expresses His Love. It is my hope that in reading this book, you have begun to learn more of the "Language of the Divine." The stories spanned from very subtle Divine guidance to profound examples of experiencing God up close and very personal. After reading this book I hope you now know your relationship with God has the potential to be more profound, more personal, and more loving than any organized religion on Earth currently teaches.

If you wish to develop a relationship with God's Prophet, seek the inner side of Prophet, for he is spiritually already with you. Few are able to meet the current physical incarnation and most people do not need to meet Prophet physically. Gently sing HU for a few minutes and then sing "Prophet" with love in your heart and he will respond. It may take time to recognize his presence, but it will come. The Light and Love that flows through him is the same that has flowed through all of God's true Prophets.

A more abundant life awaits you,

Prophet Del Hall III

Articles of Faith

Written by Prophet Del Hall III

1. There is one true God who is still living and active in our lives. He is knowable and wants a relationship with each of His children. He is the same God Jesus called FATHER and is known by many names, including Heavenly Father, and the ancient names for God, HU, and Sugmad (Pronounced SOOG-mahd). God wants a loving, trusting, personal relationship with each of us, NOT one based upon fear or guilt.

2. The Holy Spirit is God's expression in all the worlds. It is in two parts, the Light and the Sound. It is through His Holy Spirit God communicates and delivers all His gifts: peace, clarity, love, joy, healings, correction, guidance, wisdom, comfort, truth, dreams, new revelations, and more.

3. God always has a chosen living Prophet to teach His ways, speak His Living Word, lift up Souls, and bring us closer to God. God's living Prophet is a concentrated aspect of the Holy Spirit, the Light and Sound, and is raised up and

ordained by God directly. His Prophet is empowered and authorized to share God's Light and Sound and to correct misunderstandings of His ways. There are two aspects of God's Prophet, an inner spiritual and outer physical Prophet. The inner Prophet can teach us through dreams, intuition, spiritual travel, inner communication, and his presence. The outer Prophet also teaches through his discourses, written word, and his presence. There is no separation between the inner and outer Prophet. Both inner and outer aspects of Prophet are concentrated aspects of the Holy Spirit. Prophet is always with us spiritually on the inner. Prophet points to and glorifies the Father.

4. God so loves the world and His children He has always had a long unbroken line of His chosen Prophets on Earth. They existed before Jesus and after Jesus. Jesus was God's Prophet and His actual SON. God's chosen Prophets are considered to be in the "role of God's son," though NOT literally His Son. Only Jesus was literally His Son. Prophets were sometimes called Paraclete. The Bible uses the word Comforter, but the original Greek word was Paraclete, which is more accurate. Paraclete implies an actual physical person who helps, counsels,

encourages, advocates, comforts, sets free, and more.

5. Our real and eternal self is called Soul. We are Soul; we do NOT "have" a Soul. As Soul we are literally an individualized piece of God's Holy Spirit, thereby divine in nature. As an individual and uniquely experienced Soul you have free will, intelligence, imagination, opinions, clear and continuous access to Divine guidance, and immortality. As Soul we have an innate and profound spiritual growth potential. Soul has the ability to travel the Heavens spiritually with Prophet to gain truth and wisdom and grow in love. Soul exists because God loves It.

6. We have one eternal life as Soul. However, Soul needs to incarnate many times into a physical body to learn and grow spiritually mature. Soul's long journey back home to God where It was first created encompasses many lifetimes. A loving God does not expect His children to learn His ways in a single lifetime.

7. Soul equals Soul, in that God loves all Souls equally and each Soul has the same innate qualities and potential. Soul is neither male nor female, any particular race, nationality, or age. When Soul comes into a physical body at birth, the physical body is male or female, a certain

race, a nationality, and has an age. All Souls are children of God. We do not have to earn God's Love; He loves us unconditionally.

8. Soul incarnates on Earth to grow in the ability to give and receive love and learn to live the way God wishes us to live. Because God loves us, His ways of living create abundant, happy, fulfilling lives. His beautiful ways of living are mostly HOW to live, and less on what NOT to do.

9. God is more interested in two Souls learning to love one another regardless of their sexual preference. God loves you just the way you are.

10. It is God's will that a negative power exists to help Soul grow spiritually through challenges and hardships, thereby strengthening and maturing Soul. We are never given a challenge greater than our ability to find a solution to or understand the necessary lesson, if we use our God-given creativity, make sufficient personal effort, and ask for and accept the help available from the Divine. Soul has the ability to rise above any obstacles with God's help.

11. We study the Bible as an authentic teaching tool of God's ways, in addition to books and discourses authored by a Prophet chosen by God. We know the original biblical writings are

sometimes misunderstood, for example, God loves each of us regardless of our errors and shortcomings. God's eternal abandonment or damnation is not true. He would never turn His back to us for eternity. (Isaiah 54:7-8 and 10, Lamentations 3:31-32, and Hebrews 13:5)

12. Karma is the way in which the Divine accounts for our actions, words, thoughts, and attitudes. One can create positive or negative karma. Karma is a blessing used to teach us responsibility.

13. A child is not born in sin, however, the child does have karma from former lives. Karma, God's accounting system, explains our birth circumstances better than the concept of sin.

14. A living Prophet, including Jesus, can remove karma and sin when necessary to help us get started or to grow on the path home to God. However, it is primarily our responsibility to live and grow in the ways of God, thereby not creating negative karma and sin.

15. There are four commandments of God in which we abide: First — Love God with all your heart, mind, and Soul; Second — Love your neighbor as yourself. The Third is, "Seek ye first the Kingdom of God, and His righteousness."

This means that it is primarily our responsibility to draw close to God, learn His ways, and strive to live the way God would like us to live. God's Prophet is sent to show His ways. Our purpose, the Fourth Commandment, is to become spiritually mature to be used by God to bless His children. Becoming a coworker with God through His Comforter is our primary purpose in life and the most rewarding attainment of Soul.

16. All Souls upon translation, death of the physical body, go to the higher worlds, called Heavens, planes, or mansions, regardless of their beliefs. The way they live life on Earth and the effort made to draw close to God impacts the area of Heaven they are to be sent. Those who purposely harm others (except in defense of self or others), themselves, or live against the ways of God go to unpleasant locations on the first Heaven; to a location where they can learn how to do better, as a gift of love. The first Heaven has a wide range of locations, from very very unpleasant and hellish, to wonderful and beautiful places to spend time with loved ones while learning and preparing for future incarnations. Those who draw close to a Prophet of God, including Jesus, receive special care. We know of twelve distinct Heavens, not one. The

primary Abode of the Heavenly Father is in the twelfth Heaven, known as the Ocean of Love and Mercy. We can visit God while we still live on Earth, if taken by His chosen Prophet and only as Soul, not in a physical body.

17. Prayer is sacred, personal exchange with God and is an extreme privilege. God hears every prayer from the heart whether or not we recognize a response. Singing an ancient name of God, HU, is our foundational prayer. It expresses love and gratitude to God and is unencumbered by words. Singing HU has the potential to raise us up in consciousness making us more receptive to God's Love, Light, and guiding Hand. After praying it is best to spend time listening to God. Prayer should never be rote or routine. We desire to trust God and to know His will for us, and then freely and joyfully surrender to His will rather than our own will. God's Prophet can teach us the "Language of the Divine" which will help us understand how God communicates with us and help us recognize God's Love in our lives.

18. It is our responsibility to stay spiritually nourished. When Soul is nourished and fortified It becomes activated, and we are more receptive and have clearer communication with the Divine.

When Jesus said, "Give us this day our daily bread," he meant daily spiritual nourishment, not physical bread. The Holy Spirit is nourishment for Soul. This can be received by singing HU, studying Scripture, praying, dream study, demonstrating gratitude for our blessings, being in a living Prophet's physical presence or in his inner presence, or listening to his words.

19. TRUTH has the power to improve every area of our lives, but only if understood, accepted, and integrated into our lives.

20. God and His Prophet guide us in our sleeping dreams and awake dreams as a gift of love. God's Prophet teaches how to understand both types of dreams. All areas of our lives may be blessed by the wisdom God offers each of us directly in dreams.

21. Gratitude is extremely important on the path of love. It is literally the secret of love. Developing an attitude of gratitude is necessary to becoming spiritually mature. Recognizing and being grateful for the blessings of God in our lives is vital to building a loving and trusting relationship with God and His chosen Prophet. A relationship with God's Prophet is THE KEY to everything good. This includes a more abundant

life filled with the Treasures of Heaven Jesus taught about in Matthew 6.

22. We are to be good stewards of our blessings. We recognize them as gifts of love from God and make the effort to have remembrance. Remembering our blessings helps to keep our hearts open to God and builds trust in God's Love for us.

23. We give others the respect and freedom to have their own beliefs, make their own choices, and live their lives as they wish. We expect the same in return.

24. The Love and blessings of God and His Prophet are available to all who are receptive. If one desires guidance and help from Prophet, ask from the heart and sing "Prophet." He will respond. One does not need to meet Prophet physically to receive help because he is a concentrated aspect of God's Holy Spirit, and is always with us. To be taught by Prophet in the physical is a sacred blessing. Much can be gained by reading or listening to the Heavenly Father's teachings being shared by Prophet.

25. We have a responsibility to do our part and let God and His Prophet do their part. This responsibility brings freedom. Our goal is to

remain spiritually nourished, live the ways of God, live in balance with a core peace, and serve God as a coworker through His Comforter. We pray to use our God-given free will in a way that our actions, thoughts, words, and attitudes testify and bear witness to the Glory and Love of God.

26. There is always more to learn and grow in God's ways and truth. One cannot remain the same spiritually. One must make the effort to move forward or risk falling backward. To grow in consciousness and love requires change. Spiritual wisdom gained during our earthly incarnations can be taken to the other worlds when we translate, and into future lifetimes, unlike our physical possessions that remain in the physical.

Contact Information

Guidance for a Better Life is a worldwide mentoring program provided by Prophet Del Hall III and his son Del Hall IV. Personal one-on-one mentoring at our retreat center is our premier offering and the most direct and effective way to grow spiritually. Spiritual tools, guided exercises, and in-depth discourses on the eternal teachings of God are provided to help one become more aware of and receptive to His Holy Spirit and the abundance that awaits. With this personally-tailored guidance one begins to more fully recognize God's Love daily in their lives, both the dramatic and the very subtle. Over time our mentoring reduces fear, worry, anxiety, lack of purpose, feelings of unworthiness, guilt, and confusion; replacing those negative aspects of life with an abundance of peace, clarity, joy, wisdom, love, and self-respect leading to a more personal relationship with God, more than most know is possible. We also offer our videos, and more than twenty inspirational and educational books.

Guidance for a Better Life

P.O. Box 219
Lyndhurst, Virginia 22952
(540) 377-6068
contact@guidanceforabetterlife.com
www.guidanceforabetterlife.com

"A Growing Testament to the Power of God's Love One Profound Book at a Time."

If you could only read one of Prophet Del Hall's books this is the one. It is full of Keys to unlock the treasures of Heaven and bring more of God's Love into your life.

Spiritual Keys

For a More Abundant Life

PROPHET DEL HALL

Wayshowers are God's special emissaries to Earth. Our Heavenly Father loves us so much He has never left us alone without a Wayshower to teach us His true ways. This book explores the amazing history of God's chosen and ordained Wayshowers from thirty-five thousand years ago to today through specific examples of both well-known and little-known Wayshowers.

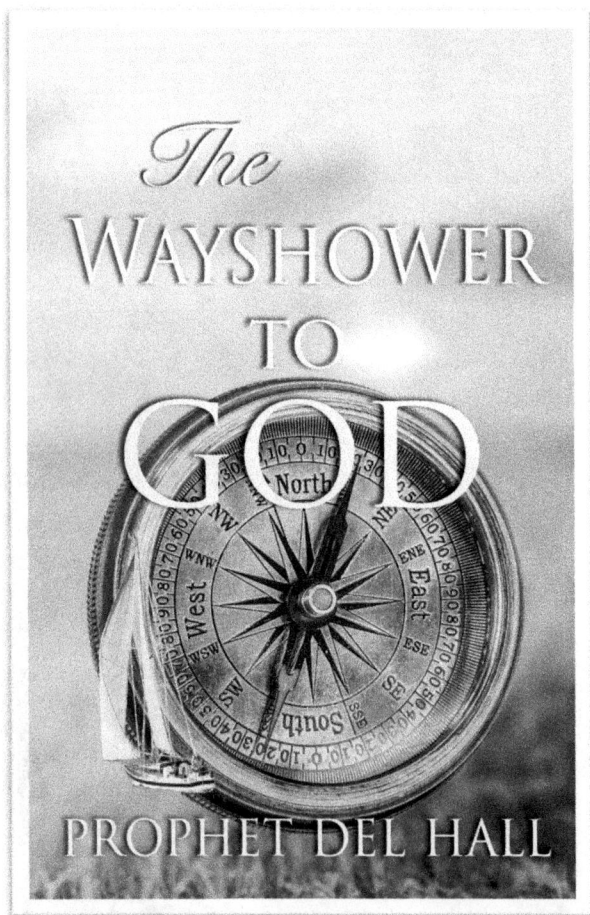

The
WAYSHOWER
TO
GOD

PROPHET DEL HALL

GOD IS IN THE GARDEN
PARABLES

Regardless of what your venture is in life you can benefit from this unassuming book. It may appear small, but the parables contained within have the power to affect your life in extraordinary ways.

GOD
IS IN THE
Garden

PARABLES
BY DEL HALL IV

ZOOM WITH PROPHET

Guidance for a Better Life retreat center has been hosting in-person mountaintop retreats at our beautiful location in the Blue Ridge Mountains of Virginia since 1990. When the pandemic began in 2020, it inspired us to get creative with how to connect with our students and new seekers. It was then our *Zoom With Prophet* meeting series was born. Some of these Zoom meetings are now being put into book form for those who could not attend.

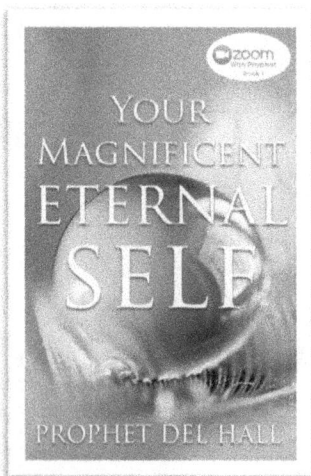

YOUR MAGNIFICENT ETERNAL SELF
PROPHET DEL HALL

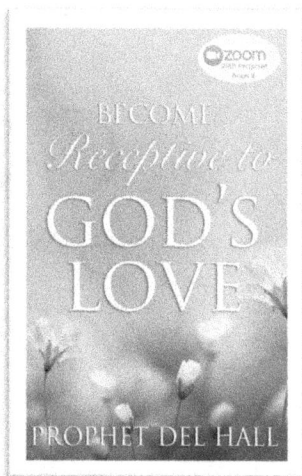

BECOME Receptive to GOD'S LOVE
PROPHET DEL HALL

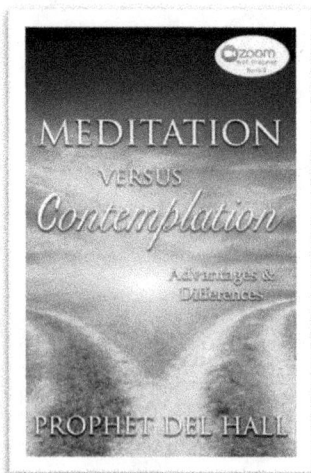

MEDITATION VERSUS Contemplation
Advantages & Differences
PROPHET DEL HALL

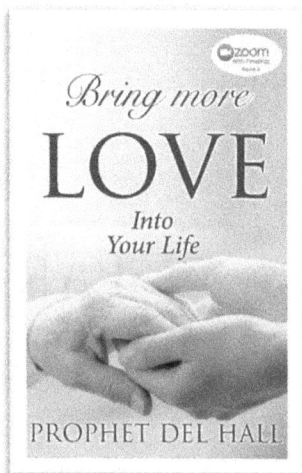

Bring more LOVE Into Your Life
PROPHET DEL HALL

SPECIALIZED TOPICS

Whether you wish to reconnect with a loved one who has passed, understand how you too can experience God's Light, improve your marriage, or learn how to understand your dreams, these incredible books have you covered.

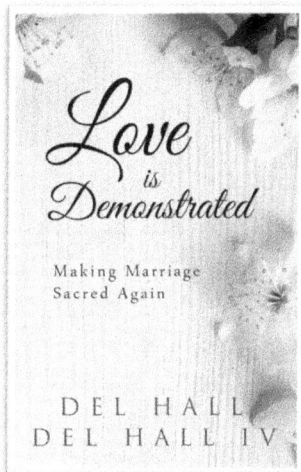

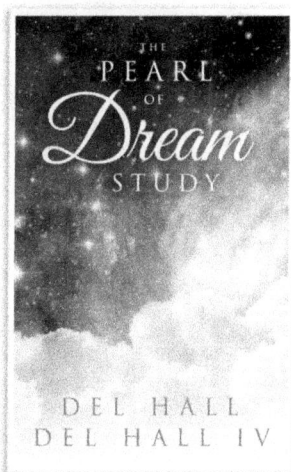

DEL HALL & DEL HALL IV

VISIT
Loved Ones
IN
HEAVEN

Prophet
Shares
God's
Light

DEL HALL & DEL HALL IV

Love
is
Demonstrated

Making Marriage
Sacred Again

DEL HALL
DEL HALL IV

THE
PEARL
OF
Dream
STUDY

DEL HALL
DEL HALL IV

TESTIMONIES OF GOD'S LOVE SERIES

God expresses His Love every day in many different and sometimes subtle ways. Often this love goes unrecognized because the ways in which God communicates are not well known. Each of the books in this series contains fifty true stories that will help you learn to better recognize the Love of God in your life.

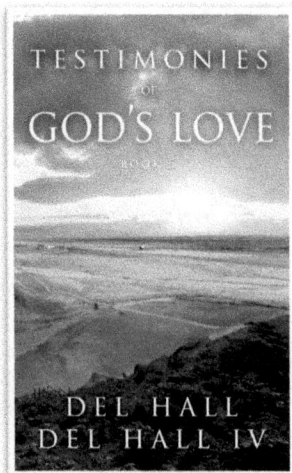

JOURNEY TO A TRUE SELF-IMAGE SERIES

This series includes intimate and unique stories that many readers will be able to personally identify with, enjoy, and learn from. They will help the reader transcend the false images people often carry about themselves — first and foremost that they are only their physical mind and body. The authors share their journeys of recognizing and coming to more fully accept their true self-image, that of Soul — an eternal child of God.

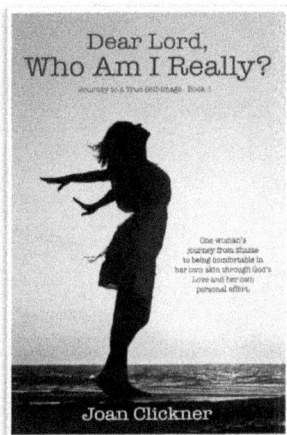

Dear Lord, Who Am I Really? — Joan Clickner

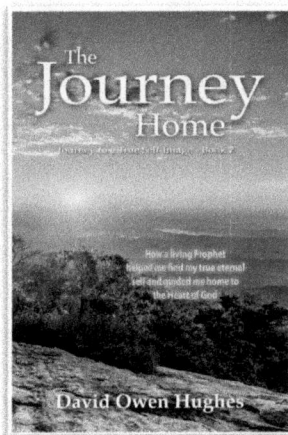

The Journey Home — David Owen Hughes

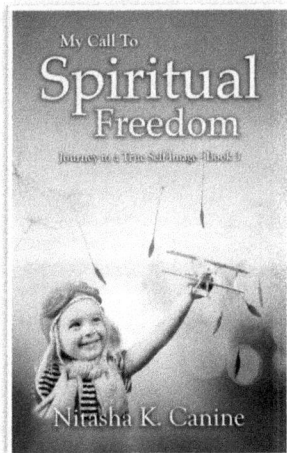

My Call To Spiritual Freedom — Nitasha K. Canine

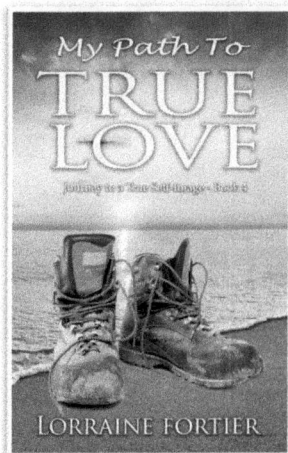

My Path To True Love — Lorraine Fortier

www.ingramcontent.com/pod-product-compliance
Lightning Source LLC
Chambersburg PA
CBHW060235050426
42448CB00009B/1453